François Boucher
in North American Collections:
100 Drawings

François Boucher
in North American Collections:
100 Drawings

Regina Shoolman Slatkin

National Gallery of Art, Washington
The Art Institute of Chicago

EXHIBITION DATES

COVER: CATALOG NUMBER 44

FRONTISPIECE: CATALOG NUMBER 40

PAGE XVI: CATALOG NUMBER 32

National Gallery of Art

December 23, 1973 through March 17, 1974

The Art Institute of Chicago

April 4, through May 12, 1974

CONTENTS

FOREWORD

We are proud to be able to hold, with The Art Institute of Chicago, this exhibition of drawings by François Boucher, the reigning artist of mid-eighteenth-century France. It is, we believe, the first major exhibition of Boucher drawings in North America, many of which have never been exhibited this side of the Atlantic. Borrowed only from collections in the United States and Canada, the drawings show the wide range of Boucher's draftsmanship and subject matter.

There are countless people to thank for their work on this exhibition. The first is certainly Regina Slatkin, who has concentrated on Boucher for some thirty years and has written both the catalog entries and the introduction. David Rust of the National Gallery's staff assisted in preparing the catalog and is responsible for the somewhat expanded Washington exhibition which stresses the various aspects of Boucher's oeuvre and encompassing influence. We are also grateful to Harold Joachim, Curator of Drawings at The Art Institute of Chicago, who, with Mr. Rust, selected the drawings and has been invaluable in the organization of our joint effort.

We are also fortunate to have had the encouragement and cooperation of Mrs. Helen Regenstein, who made possible the acquisition of so many outstanding French drawings at The Art Institute. We wish also to express our warm thanks to Phyllis Lambert and Belle Linsky for their generous support of the production of the entire exhibition catalog.

Foremost in my mind are the lenders who have been so enormously generous. Except for two drawings already committed to other exhibitions, every loan request was granted. For this we want to express our deep indebtedness to the trustees, directors and curators of all the lending institutions, and to the private collectors who have parted with their drawings for so many months. It is they who have made possible this celebration of one of the great draftsmen of the western tradition.

J. Carter Brown
Director

ACKNOWLEDGMENTS

Some twenty-five years ago, a grant from the Bollingen Foundation enabled me to start gathering material for a study of François Boucher's work. This catalog of Boucher drawings in North American collections is an outgrowth of the comprehensive study, still in progress, of the artist's oeuvre. For the initial help toward my project, my sincerest thanks go to the Bollingen Foundation, and especially to Huntington Cairns, whose sympathetic understanding gave me the impetus to begin my task.

Over the years, many friends have given me their support in this undertaking, foremost among them three women whose taste and knowledge did much to further my own interest in the eighteenth century: Therese K. Straus, Saidye R. Bronfman and Helen Regenstein. I am deeply indebted also to a number of scholars who helped me to gain valuable insights into specialized areas of art history: A. Hyatt Mayor, Curator Emeritus of Prints, The Metropolitan Museum of Art; Sir Francis Watson, Director, Wallace Collection; Edith A. Standen, Curatorial Consultant, The Metropolitan Museum of Art; Léo Bronstein, art historian; Elizabeth E. Roth, Curator, Print Division, New York Public Library, and the late director of the Philadelphia Museum of Art, Fiske Kimball, whose work on eighteenth century French ornamental design revealed so much new and fascinating material.

To Jean Adhémar, Conservateur en Chef, and M. Barbin, Conservateur, Cabinet des Estampes, Bibliothèque Nationale; to Jean-Pierre Babelon, Conservateur en Chef and Mireille Rambeaud, Conservateur, Archives Nationales, Paris, I should like to express my gratitude for permission to study certain material and documents in the reserve section of the Bibliothèque Nationale and the archives of the Minutier Central.

I have been fortunate in having the unfailing cooperation of the staff of the Cabinet des Dessins of the Louvre. For the kindness they have always extended to me, I should like to thank Maurice Sérullaz, Conservateur en Chef; Roseline Bacou, Conservateur des Musées Nationaux; Lise Duclaux, Conservateur and Geneviève Monnier, Conservateur, all of the Cabinet des Dessins. My friend Geneviève Monnier, especially, has earned my gratitude, for on the frequent occasions when I requested her help, she always responded promptly and graciously.

Many curators of the French provincial museums have enabled me to study the drawings of François Boucher in their collections, although this often entailed additional work for them and their staff. D. Ojalvo, Conservateur du Musée des Beaux-Arts, Orléans, and L. M. Cornillot, Conservateur du Musée des Beaux-Arts, Besançon, went to great lengths to secure for me access to their collections at a time more convenient to me than to them, and for this I render my thanks. Pierrette Jean-Richard, Conservateur, Collection Edmond de Rothschild, has made available to me the wealth of material housed in that splendid collection, and has clarified for me many obscure points concerning prints by and after Boucher. Jean Cailleux has not only shared with me his extensive knowledge of eighteenth century French art, but has supplied me, time and again with much-needed photographs and information. To him, and to Marianne Michel who years ago helped me to catalog the vast collection of prints after Boucher in the Cabinet des Estampes of the Bibliothèque Nationale, go my warmest thanks. I am also obliged to Mme Bouleau-Rabaud of the Ecole Nationale des Beaux-Arts, Paris, for allowing me to examine the registers of the Académie Royale, and to Madeleine Jarry of the Mobilier National for elucidating certain points concerning Boucher's designs for the Gobelins tapestries.

As much as anything, the encouragement of certain scholars who were always willing to talk to me about my work, has often helped me to sustain my interest. By confronting me with problems, questions of attribution and works heretofore unknown, they challenged me to probe further into the accumulation of art-historical data which has grown up around Boucher's oeuvre in the last two and half centuries. Thus I am indebted to my friendly interlocutors: Agnes Mongan, Director Emeritus of the Fogg Art Museum; Anita Brookner of the Courtauld Institute; E. Haverkamp-Begemann, History of Art Department, Yale University; Per Bjurström, Curator of Drawings, Nationalmuseum, Stockholm, and chiefly, the late Frits Lugt, whose questions and answers were equally stimulating.

The curators of our own museums have not only been generous with loans but with the time they placed at my disposal on frequent occasions, when I came to discuss those loans. My indebtedness is great to Harold Joachim, Curator of Prints and Drawings, The Art Institute of Chicago, one of the organizers of this exhibition; to Jacob Bean, Curator of Drawings, Linda Gillies, Assistant Curator and John J. McKendry, Curator of Prints, The Metropolitan Museum of Art; Felice Stampfle, Curator of Drawings, The Pierpont Morgan Library; Eleanor Sayre, Curator of Prints, Museum of Fine Arts, Boston; Alan Shestack, Director, Yale University Art Gallery; James K. Kettlewell, Curator, The Hyde Collection; Elaine Dee, Curator of Prints and Drawings, Cooper-Hewitt Museum of Decorative Arts and Design; Jean Sutherland Boggs, Director and Mary C. Taylor, Curator of Drawings, The National Gallery of Canada; Phyllis Hattis, Visiting Curator, California Palace of the Legion of Honor, who was good enough to examine and photograph for me the drawings by Boucher in the Crocker Gallery at Sacramento. David Rust of the National Gallery of Art participated in the organization of this exhibition from its inception, patiently helping me to surmount any difficulties that arose and editing the catalog with painstaking care. He also managed, after much sleuthing, to discover the whereabouts of one of the most attractive drawings in the exhibition, which had been lost sight of for many years.

It goes without saying that no catalog of this kind, to say nothing of a complete corpus, could have been undertaken without the resources of the Frick Art Reference Library and the Witt Library in London, to whose staff, and in particular Mildred Steinbach and Helen Sanger of the Frick Library, and Christopher Wright of the Witt Library, I express my deep gratitude. Being able to study the prints and drawings in the Print Room of The British Museum was of great value to me, and for permission to do so, I wish to thank John Gere and P. H. Hulton. My knowledge of Boucher drawings was further enriched by studying the superb collections of the Rijksmuseum, the Albertina and The Hermitage, and for this privilege I wish to thank K. G. Boon, Eckhart Knab and Y. I. Kuznetsov.

I am aware of the endless hours spent on my behalf by various dealers and private collectors who not only consented to lend their drawings, but consulted their files to provide us with necessary documentation and were most generous in supplying us with photographs. I should like to make grateful mention of Roy Fisher, Eric Stiebel, and the late Georges Wildenstein.

Since many of the themes which Boucher treated dealt with classical subjects, I was glad to have the assistance of two young Harvard classicists, Laura Slatkin and Amy Johnson, to guide me through the realms of classical literature. To Carole Slatkin I am grateful for the critical reading of the text and for many useful suggestions connected with problems of iconography. My final acknowledgment is to my husband, Charles E. Slatkin, for whose firm support in every aspect of this undertaking I shall always be grateful.

Regina Shoolman Slatkin

LENDERS TO THE EXHIBITION

Mr. and Mrs. Gerald Bronfman
Estate of Walter C. Baker
Mr. and Mrs. John Canaday
Page Cross
David Daniels
Mrs. Winston F. C. Guest
Michael Hall
The Armand Hammer Foundation
Mr. and Mrs. Henry F. Harrison
S. Kramarsky Trust Fund
Mrs. Richard Krautheimer
Mr. and Mrs. Bernard Lande
Arthur L. Liebman
The Lazarus & Rosalie Phillips Family Collection
Mr. and Mrs. Joseph Verner Reed
Norbert L. H. Roesler
Arthur Ross
David Rust
Mr. and Mrs. Robert Scheiner
Mr. and Mrs. Lenard M. Shavick
Carole Slatkin
Laura Slatkin
Mr. and Mrs. Donald S. Stralem
Mrs. Herbert N. Straus
Suida-Manning Collection
Mr. and Mrs. Howard Weingrow
Wolf Collection

Rear Admiral and Mrs. Hubert Chanler
Anonymous lenders
The William Hayes Ackland Memorial Art Center,
University of North Carolina, Chapel Hill
Albright-Knox Art Gallery, Buffalo
The Art Institute of Chicago
Achenbach Foundation for Graphic Arts, California Palace of
the Legion of Honor, San Francisco
Sterling and Francine Clark Art Institute, Williamstown
The Cleveland Museum of Art
Cooper-Hewitt Museum of Decorative Arts and Design,
Smithsonian Institution, New York
E. B. Crocker Art Gallery, Sacramento
The Detroit Institute of Arts
Fogg Art Museum, Harvard University, Cambridge
The Hyde Collection, Glens Falls, New York
Indiana University Art Museum, Bloomington
The Metropolitan Museum of Art, New York
The Pierpont Morgan Library, New York
The Museum of Art, Rhode Island School of Design, Providence
Museum of Fine Arts, Boston
National Gallery of Art, Washington
The National Gallery of Canada, Ottawa
Nelson Gallery-Atkins Museum, Kansas City
The St. Louis Art Museum
The University of Iowa Museum of Art, Iowa City
The University of Michigan Museum of Art, Ann Arbor
Yale University Art Gallery, New Haven

INTRODUCTION

For François Boucher, illusion was the ultimate reality. Whatever he observed, he recorded with insight and accuracy, be it landscape, nude or scene of everyday life. But he also invested everything with a quality of make-believe, as though, gazing through the keyhole of his imagination, he glimpsed another, illusory world, more poignantly beautiful and far more satisfying than the real. In the countryside near Beauvais, Blois and Charenton he sketched landscapes *d'après nature,* but often added imaginary towers, water mills, dovecotes, stone bridges, marble fountains and flower-filled urns which lent an air of enchantment to these landscapes, turning them (sometimes literally) into stage sets against which his nymphs, gods and goddesses, shepherds and courtiers played their eternal charades. Nature became *"un thème ou un prétexte pour la fantaisie ou la brosse de l'artiste."*

The models that Boucher drew from life were real—the O'Murphy sisters, or his own wife—but they were not merely nudes: they were figures clothed in dazzling nudity. When he portrayed himself in his studio with wife, child and apprentices, he chose an imaginary setting, a seventeenth century humble Dutch interior, so as to act out a role. When he illustrated Molière's plays (in the sumptuous edition of 1734) he dressed the characters in contemporary clothes rather than the seventeenth century costumes of Molière's day, propelling the present backward into the past and mingling, as it were, with Molière's characters on the stage. Molière's realm became his own; reality became illusion.

Like Watteau's dream world, Boucher's was deeply rooted in life. His drawings are first-hand observations of the life around him: a model in the studio or at the Ecole Royale where he taught; his children, sleeping or playing; hawkers in the street crying their wares; an elegant company picnicking; a goat, a donkey, a rooster flapping his wings; a young boy holding a portfolio of sketches; a valet serving breakfast. From Watteau he learned to seize a gesture, drape a cloak, arrange a lady's coiffure. His drawings reveal minute attention to detail, adherence to living form. When he turned to Biblical subjects as he did intermittently throughout his life, it was his drawings that revealed the initial concept, the gradual evolution of the theme. Thus his drawings were the reality; his paintings the consummate dream.

Avidly collected during his own lifetime, Boucher's drawings are today dispersed among museums and private collections throughout the world. Their total hardly exceeds a thousand in number—a far cry from the ten thousand traditionally ascribed to him. He is judged by his major achievements: the great mythological cycles in the Wallace Collection and in the Louvre, in Stockholm and Tours, in Angers and Nancy and San Francisco; the pastorales in Boston, San Diego and the Metropolitan Museum; the landscapes in Toledo, Kansas City and Cincinnati; the portraits in Munich, London and Washington; the decorative ensembles in the Hôtel de Soubise, the Banque de France, the châteaux of Versailles and Fontainebleau; the tapestries in the Gobelins Museum, the Quirinale Palace, the Royal Collection in Stockholm, the Metropolitan Museum, the Philadelphia Museum, the Huntington Collection in San Marino and the *chinoiserie* designs in Besançon; the splendid group of paintings in The Frick Collection and The Hermitage.

Such are the images invoked by those who see Boucher not as a decorator but as an artist whose contribution to the mainstream of French painting is real and lasting. Is it possible to estimate this contribution by considering only a limited part of his achievement—his drawings—and even delimiting this aspect of his work still further by referring only to those drawings which are in public and private collections in North

America? Can a survey of this material chart the course of his development, tracing the evolution of his work from early tentative effort through maturity and eventual decline?

A fourth of all extant drawings by Boucher are in North American collections today. Assembled over many years, they were chosen for their high quality, their relation to key works by the artist, or their importance in illustrating a style which dominated a major part of the eighteenth century. Boucher's entire repertoire is here: portraits, landscapes, genre scenes and pastorales, nudes, children and animals, mythologies and religious compositions, designs for tapestries, fountains and clocks, architectural decorations and book illustrations. Every medium which he essayed on paper is also found here: the nervous pen and ink drawings; brush and wash; the classic *trois crayons;* black chalk heightened with white on blue, green, gray or buff paper; pen and india ink on prepared paper; pastels, and his favorite sanguine or red chalk; some brush drawings are done in monochrome or *grisaille;* frequently several techniques are combined to produce a richer effect.

Whatever the category, there are unsurpassed examples in North American collections. No landscapes by Boucher are finer than those in The Art Institute of Chicago, The Pierpont Morgan Library, the Yale University Art Gallery, the Museum of Fine Arts, Boston (Forsyth Wickes Collection).

The nudes are often studies from life, keenly observed and brilliantly executed; many are preliminary studies for Boucher's most important paintings.[1] More than half the drawings in North American collections are, in fact, directly connected with painted compositions, projects for tapestries, prints or book illustrations. Because of this, they are either dated or datable, or so well documented that they help to clarify the chronology of Boucher's work and trace his development as an artist.

The life studies are not merely circumstantial evidence; they definitely disprove the oft-quoted, disparaging statement made by Sir Joshua Reynolds in his *Tenth Discourse* (Dec. 10, 1784), in which he chided Boucher for neglecting the study of the human figure and painting his nudes from memory, instead of drawing from life. "Our neighbours, the French," Sir Joshua told the students of the Royal Academy, "are much in this practice of *extempore* invention, and their dexterity is such as even to excite admiration, if not envy; but how rarely can this praise be given to their finished pictures! . . . The late director of their academy, Boucher, was eminent in this way. When I visited him some years since, in France, I found him at work on a very large picture, without drawing or models of any kind. On my remarking this particular circumstance, he said when he was young, studying his art, he found it necessary to use models, but he had left them off for many years," and Sir Joshua added disapprovingly, "such pictures as this, was, [*sic*] and I fear always will be, produced by those who work solely from practice or memory...."

When Sir Joshua visited Boucher, in the autumn of 1752, the latter was at work on the very paintings (now in the Wallace Collection) for which so many studies from life actually do exist.[2] Was Boucher trying to impress his English colleague, or was he merely having a little fun at his expense? Or had the life studies actually become memory images which he could recall at will? The ease and fluency with which he painted give no hint of the careful planning that went into his complex decorative schemes. For instance, *The Birth of Venus* (pl. 54) is the initial concept for an elaborately designed painting for which a series of detailed studies exist, among them the *Nude* in the collection of Baron Robert von Hirsch, and the *Reclining Nude* in The British Museum. These drawings permit us to follow the process by which the artist formulated his ideas, and to see clearly how he made use of life studies in composing his pictorial schemes.

The life studies attest the fact that Boucher made, despite Sir Joshua's statement, constant use of models; in the genesis of his works the drawings from life were the intermediate step between the initial idea rendered visual, and the final realization of a complete pictorial scheme. One cannot assume, however, that all the life studies were conceived as preliminary drawings for paintings; perhaps the academic nudes in classic studio poses constituted part of a rich repository upon which Boucher drew freely. One wonders, for instance, whether the *Apollo* (pl. 68) which bears the stamp of the *Académie de Dessein d'Orléans,* was not an exceptionally fine academic drawing of a male nude done from a model at the academy for the benefit of the students, and subsequently used for the figure of the Sun God in the tapestry design. In the figure of Mercury (pl. 50), on the other hand, Boucher seems to have had the specific composition well in mind before making the model assume a pose appropriate to the cloud-borne messenger of the gods.

When an important composition was projected, the life studies were often done after the design had been mapped out; some of the preliminary sketches containing many figures were at first freely drawn, almost flung on paper, as it were, like the red and black chalk drawing of *Diana Attended by Her Nymphs* (pl. 49), the initial design for the painting *Diana after the Bath* in the Louvre, for which the study of a nude in the Walter Baker Collection was probably a later, detailed study, done from life (pl. 46). The painting *Vertumnus and Pomona* in the Louvre which was woven as a Gobelins tapestry has as its basis a highly finished drawing in The Hyde Collection (pl. 84), but the project undoubtedly originated with an earlier concept of the theme, possibly the sketch in the Hoover Collection (fig. 44), for which life studies probably existed. Often Boucher's drawings of nudes, with their solid plasticity, would undergo a complete transformation from life studies to almost abstract patterns, figures done in lively, sinuous contours, performing a purely decorative function. Freed of a need to be three-dimensional, separate elements could be recombined, as in the case of the *Three Nymphs* (pl. 63), to form a new pattern, the graceful, flowing bodies woven into an intricate arabesque.

Although Boucher treated a rich variety of subjects, a major part of his work is devoted to mythological themes. Like his contemporaries, perhaps even more so, he used the myths of classical antiquity to devise allegories which were allusions to contemporary events, lending, at times, new meaning to time-worn themes. Why did the eighteenth century, an age of rationalism, continue to make constant use of the pagan myths—Boucher's favorite subject matter? It is a question often debated;[3] like Diderot's *Neveu de Rameau,* Boucher might have said, "C'est le sentiment et le langage de toute la société." Perhaps, because the myths were allowably irrational, having been assimilated into the culture of the period, they could be used to explain the irrational elements in life— love, for instance.

The theatre was another outlet for the irrational as it affected the reality of everyday life. The Pygmalion myth, for example, became the subject of an opera-ballet, a pictorial theme and a philosophical concept (the dialogue between reality and illusion). Boucher's connection with the theatre was close and constant. He designed stage sets and costumes for the Opéra and the Opéra-Comique (Lully's *Persée* and *Athys,* Rameau's *Les Indes Galantes, Sylvie, Titon and Aurora*), and for the popular theatre of the Foire St. Laurent. Since many outstanding personalities of the theatre were his close friends—Charles Favart, playwright and director of the Opéra-Comique, and his actress-wife, Marie Duronceray, the toast of Paris; Jean Monnet, director of the Foire St. Laurent theatre, among others—Boucher was forever involved in the make-believe world of stage and country-fair, opera and ballet. The mannered poses of so many of his figures, the "artificial" landscapes, the many *Fêtes* scenes, the *Fragments d'Opéra,* the direct transcriptions of musical themes in drawings like *La Danse Allemande* (pl. 95), reflect the illusory quality of the make-believe world around him.

Among the projects which Boucher attempted time and again, until the very end of his days, were religious subjects. Few such projects were carried out. He began with a huge composition which had been prescribed by the Académie Royale: *The Deliverance of Joachim by Evilmérodach.* On this obscure theme the young Boucher, barely twenty, managed to do a handsome picture in the baroque manner which won for him the first prize at the Académie in 1723. Perhaps it was this painting[4] which convinced him that he must try to become a *peintre d'histoire sacrée,* the most distinguished title to be obtained at the Académie. Among the projects he eventually carried out was the altarpiece of an *Adoration* which he did for Madame de Pompadour's chapel at the Château de Bellevue in 1750;[5] the *Saint John Preaching;*[6] the

Infant Christ and Saint John;[7] the *Rest on the Flight;*[8] the *Virgin and Child*[9] and *Saint Anne Teaching the Virgin;*[10] less than a score of religious paintings by Boucher exist, as against the 200 recorded drawings of religious subjects.

Some of the drawings on Old and New Testament themes which Boucher did, he gave away; others he kept in his studio until he died, refusing to part with them; at the sale of his effects (Feb. 18, 1771), it was his fellow artists who acquired them, and who went on buying them in subsequent auction sales. Those which found their way into American collections are of the highest quality: *Moses Receiving the Tablets of the Law* [(pl. 3)], recorded in the sale catalog of Boucher's effects; *Hagar and Ishmael in the Desert; An Angel Feeding a Holy Hermit,* the only drawing by Boucher which his pupil Fragonard etched; the *Adoration of the Shepherds* (pl. 67), related to the Bellevue altarpiece; the *Baptism of Christ* in Saint Louis (pl. 6); *Christ and the Woman Taken in Adultery* in the Metropolitan Museum (pl. 7), and the Cleveland *Presentation in the Temple* (pl. 99), a variant of the *Presentation* in the Cabinet des Dessins, Louvre, one of the very last drawings Boucher did before his death.

These drawings demonstrate the various ways in which Boucher strove to make a personal statement about a subject that preoccupied him most of his active life: to paint a devotional picture of high seriousness. It was a statement rejected by most of his contemporary critics who found his manner too casual, his Madonnas too worldly, his vision too mundane. Yet, in a way, the religious drawings became his most personal statement, done not as commissions, not even (aside from some very early work) as illustrations, but as constant attempts to find a solution to a problem he had posed himself.

The art historian Léo Bronstein once remarked that Boucher's obsession (to understand an artist, you must discover his obsession!) was the baby. Who thinks of innocence in context with Boucher? Sensuous is the term most frequently applied to his work, and his nudes are thought of as sex symbols in a libertine age. Diderot's harsh judgment, "This man has everything, except honesty", was echoed many times by those who were more concerned with the subject matter of his work than with the work itself.

Is it really naive to suggest that Boucher's obsession was the baby? Perhaps not. His women rarely mature; their bodies remain dimpled and rosy like those of infants. It was his seventeen-year-old wife and the king's fifteen-year-old mistress who served most often as the models for Venus and Diana whom he painted and drew in all the freshness and radiance of youth, showing them not merely as nudes, but as eternally young bodies, boldly innocent, with the innocence of childhood.

Babies and children are ever present in Boucher's work, as they undoubtedly were in his real life, for he had three children of his own, and several young apprentices. He drew and painted them innumerable times—babies asleep and awake, playful, shy, sulking, tumbling about or nestling against their mothers. They were the winged cherubs in his *Adorations,* the *amoretti* in his mythologies, the genii in his allegories. As they grew older, the infants of his household were shown at their games and pastimes, and his boy apprentices at the serious business of learning their trade. The *Sleeping Infant* (pl. 10), like the sleeping infants in the Nationalmuseum, Stockholm, and the *Two Children* (pl. 9), the *Baby* in the Boymans Museum and the *Boy Drinking from a Bowl* (pl. 11) are convincing life studies, undoubtedly done after his own children. He was to include these studies of children in his paintings, long after his son and daughters were grown.

It is possible to establish a complete chronological sequence of Boucher's drawings from the examples found in North American collections. The early self-portrait, done about 1724, shows his dependence on Watteau, whose corpus of drawings he etched; the figure of *Aurora* whose youthful charms recall those of the seventeen-year-old Jeanne Buseau whom Boucher had married in 1733, is a study for the painting at Nancy, done that same year. The *Seated Lady* in the Reed Collection (pl. 22) and the *Seated Lady* in the Metropolitan Museum (pl. 23), both done about 1736, recall the crisp, dashing manner of the Molière illustrations; the *Seated Male Nude* (pl. 24), dated 1738, shows Boucher at his academic best, as does the *Reclining Nude* (pl. 35), done that same year. The *Boy Holding a Carrot* (pl. 32) and the *Valet* (pl. 36) mark the emergence of Boucher's more personal, individual style, culminating in the landscape drawings of the forties, the mythological cycles and portraits of the fifties. The studies of the hands for the portrait of Madame de Pompadour can be dated 1756; the *Venus with a Dove* (pl. 75) is dated 1757; to the sixties belong the *Diploma of the Freemasons* (pl. 85), the *Design for a Clock* (pl. 86) and the illustrations for the edition of Ovid published in 1767. *The Presentation in the Temple* (pl. 99) exemplifies the loose, overwrought manner of his last efforts.

The inexhaustible versatility with which Boucher improvised his themes is surely best conveyed by his drawings. For almost a century Americans have collected some of the finest examples, many of which are here exhibited for the first time. Many famous European collections have yielded up their treasures: Randon de Boisset; Stainville; Sireuil; d'Argenville; Reynolds, Rogers, Warwick; Heseltine, Chennevières, Marmontel, Montesquiou-Fezenzac; Masson, Paulme, Wauters, Coblentz, The Hermitage, Groult and David-Weill are the distinguished collectors' names that recur in the provenance of these drawings. Some of the most beautiful drawings have no known provenance but were simply acquired by discerning collectors and curators because of their quality.

North American institutions and private collectors have been generous with loans, and Boucher drawings have recrossed the Atlantic to be shown in exhibitions in London, Paris, Amsterdam, Rotterdam, Florence and other European cities. In the United States and Canada they have been seen in a great many museum and university exhibitions, studied, discussed and appreciated by scholars and by the general public.

The scope of this exhibition is of necessity limited, including less than half the drawings by Boucher in our collections. Some examples were omitted despite their excellence, in order to allow for greater variety; others, like the superb group in the Forsyth Wickes Collection at the Museum of Fine Arts, Boston, were not available for exhibition purposes because of restrictions in the bequest. But if the field of vision is narrowed, the objects stand out in sharper focus. It is important to emphasize, by choosing the finest drawings, Boucher's excellence as a draftsman; but it is also necessary to show him as an artist thinking with his pen and crayon, feeling with his brush. Thus the showpieces have sometimes been omitted in favor of the tentative sketch, the pretty pastel nude in favor of a somber religious subject. Because of their private, intimate character, Boucher's drawings best reveal his links with the past, the sources upon which he drew. The relevance of his works in the future will lie not in the outworn themes of his subject matter, but in the high standards of his draftsmanship, the unremitting discipline he imposed upon himself even in the humblest task. These are the elements that must insure their survival.

Regina Shoolman Slatkin

1. The *Aurora* (pl. 20) is a study for the painting *Aurora and Cephalus* in the Musée des Beaux-Arts, Nancy; the *Seated Nude* (pl. 34) in the Albright-Knox Gallery is a study for one of the *Three Graces* which Boucher painted for the Hôtel de Soubise and which exists, in another version, in the Gulbenkian Foundation, Lisbon; the *Reclining Nude* (pl. 35) in the Fogg Art Museum is the figure of Venus in *Venus and Mars,* in the Los Angeles County Museum; the *Valet* in The Art Institute of Chicago (pl. 36) is a study for the Louvre picture *Le Déjeuner;* the *Mercury* in the Daniels Collection is a study for *Mercury Confiding the Infant Bacchus to the Nymphs* in the Wallace Collection (pl. 50); the beautiful study of a female nude (pl. 66) is the nymph in the foreground of the painting *Apollo and Issé* in the Museum at Tours; the *Reclining Nude* (pl. 79) is the nymph Syrinx in the painting *Pan and Syrinx* in the National Gallery, London; the *Apollo* (pl. 68) is a study for *The Rising of the Sun* in the Wallace Collection; the *Minerva* (pl. 71) is a life study for the goddess Minerva in the Wallace Collection's *Judgment of Paris.*

2. In his biography of Reynolds, E. K. Waterhouse writes: "He left Rome on 3rd May, 1752, and was in England by the middle of October in the same year, spending a month in Paris, where he painted two portraits and learned to despise the French School." (E. K. Waterhouse, *Reynolds,* London, 1941, p. 8).

3. J. Seznec, *The Survival of the Pagan Gods,* trans. B. F. Sessions, Bollingen Series 38, New York, 1953.

4. Boucher's first important picture is now in the Columbia Museum of Art, South Carolina (Samuel H. Kress Collection).

5. Now in the Musée des Beaux-Arts, Lyon.

6. Molesworth Collection, London.

7. Uffizi.

8. Hermitage.

9. The Metropolitan Museum of Art.

10. Phoenix Art Museum.

BIBLIOGRAPHY CITED IN ABBREVIATED FORM

Ananoff	Ananoff, A. *L'Oeuvre dessiné de François Boucher*. I. Paris, 1966.
Apollo	Slatkin, R. "Portraits of François Boucher." *Apollo*, Oct. 1971, pp. 280–291.
Bacou	Bacou, R. "Quimper: dessins du Musée des Beaux-Arts." *Revue de l'Art*, no. 14, 1971.
Badin	Badin, J. *La Manufacture de Tapisseries de Beauvais*, Paris, 1909.
Baudicour	Baudicour, P. de. *Le Peintre-graveur français continué*. 2 vols. Paris, 1859–1861.
Carlson, 1966	Carlson, V. "Three Drawings by François Boucher." *Master Drawings, 4*, no. 2, 1966.
Goncourt	Goncourt, E. and J. de. *L'Art du dix-huitième siècle*. I. Paris, 1880.
Heseltine, 1900	*Drawings by François Boucher, J. H. Fragonard and Antoine Watteau in the Collection of J. P. Heseltine.* London, 1900.
Heseltine, 1913	*Dessins de l'école française du dix-huitième siècle provenant de la collection H. . . .* Text by L. Guiraud. Paris, 1913.
Levey	Kalnein, Graf F. W., and Levey, M. *Art and Architecture of the Eighteenth Century in France.* Baltimore, 1972.
Jean-Richard	Jean-Richard, P. *François Boucher, gravures et dessins provenant du Cabinet des Dessins et de la Collection Edmond de Rothschild au Musée du Louvre.* Paris, 1971.
Leymarie	Leymarie, L. de. *L'Oeuvre de Gilles Demarteau l'Ainé, graveur du roi.* Paris, 1896.
Lugt	Lugt, F. *Les Marques de collections de dessins & d'estampes. . . .* Amsterdam, 1921; *Supplément,* The Hague, 1956.
Michel	Michel, A. *François Boucher. Catalogue raisonné de l'Oeuvre peint et dessiné.* Catalog by L. Soullié and C. Masson. Paris, n.d. [1906].

Pigler   Pigler, A. *Barockthemen.* 2 vols. Budapest, 1956.

Rosenberg   Rosenberg, P. *French Master Drawings of the 17th & 18th Centuries in North American Collections.* [Exhibition catalog for Toronto, Ottawa, San Francisco and New York.] London, 1972.

Popham and Fenwick   Popham, A. E. and Fenwick, K. M. *European Drawings in the Collection of the National Gallery of Canada.* Toronto, 1965.

Portalis   Portalis, R. *Les Dessinateurs d'illustration au dix-huitième siècle.* 2 vols. Paris, 1877.

Shoolman and Slatkin   Shoolman, R. and Slatkin, C. E. *Six Centuries of French Master Drawings in America.* New York, 1950.

Slatkin, 1967   Slatkin, R. S., Review of A. Ananoff, *L'Oeuvre dessiné de François Boucher. Master Drawings, 5,* no. 1, 1967, pp. 54–66.

Slatkin, 1972   Slatkin, R. S. "Some Boucher Drawings and Related Prints." *Master Drawings, 10,* no. 3, 1972, pp. 264–283.

Vallery-Radot   Vallery-Radot, J. *French Drawings, 15th Century through Géricault.* New York, 1964.

EXHIBITIONS CITED IN ABBREVIATED FORM

Boucher, 1932 | Paris, Hôtel Charpentier, "Exposition François Boucher," 1932.

Boucher, 1957 | New York, Charles E. Slatkin Galleries, "François Boucher, an Exhibition of Prints and Drawings," 1957.

Daniels Collection, 1968 | The Minneapolis Institute of Arts; The Art Institute of Chicago; Kansas City, Nelson Gallery-Atkins Museum; Cambridge, Fogg Art Museum, "Drawings from the Daniels Collection," 1968. Catalog by M. L. Bennett and A. Mongan.

London, Royal Academy, 1968 | London, Royal Academy of Arts, "France in the Eighteenth Century," 1968.

Paris, Orangerie, 1958 | Paris, Musée de l'Orangerie, "De Clouet à Matisse," and Rotterdam, Museum Boymans, "Van Clouet tot Matisse," 1958; New York, The Metropolitan Museum of Art, "French Drawings from American Collections, Clouet to Matisse," 1959.

San Francisco, 1940 | San Francisco, Golden Gate International Exposition, "Master Drawings," 1940.

Slatkin, 1959 | New York, Charles E. Slatkin Galleries, "French Master Drawings, A Loan Exhibition," 1959.

Toronto, Ottawa, San Francisco, New York, 1972–73 | Toronto, Art Gallery of Ontario; Ottawa, The National Gallery of Canada; San Francisco, California Palace of the Legion of Honor; New York, The New York Cultural Center, "French Master Drawings of the 17th & 18th Centuries in North American Collections," 1972–73. Catalog by P. Rosenberg.

Wildenstein, 1963 | New York, Wildenstein, "Master Drawings from The Art Institute of Chicago," 1963.

CATALOG

I
Early Self-Portrait
Red and black chalk heightened with white
115 x 92
Provenance: A. Mouriau (Lugt 1829, 1853; sale, Paris, Mar.
11, 1858, no. 322)
Bibliography: Apollo, 1971, pp. 285–286, fig. 22
Lent anonymously

The *Early Self-Portrait,* while cataloged in the Mouriau Sale as by Watteau, has been identified as Boucher's self-portrait,[1] done when he was about twenty-two. The basis for this identification is the young man's unmistakable resemblance to several portraits of Boucher, including the Louvre painting, *L'Artiste dans son atelier* (fig. 1) done when Boucher was about twenty, and Gustave Lundberg's well-known portrait of Boucher at forty (fig. 2), also in the Louvre.

Boucher's first important commission was given to him by Watteau's patron Jean de Julienne: to participate in etching the corpus of Watteau's drawings, known as *Figures de différents caractères.* For this work which appeared in two volumes (1726 and 1728), Boucher etched over 100 plates, a task which so influenced his draftsmanship that it bore, especially at the beginning of his career, the indelible imprint of Watteau's style. It is to this period, before Boucher left on his journey to Italy (1727–1731), that the early self-portrait belongs.

1. *Apollo,* 1971, pp. 285-286.

Fig. 2. Lundberg. *Portrait of Boucher.*
Pastel. Paris, Musée du Louvre

Fig. 1. *Artist in His Studio.*
Painting. Paris, Musée du Louvre

Mucius Scaevola before King Lars Porsenna

Black chalk heightened with white on blue paper
465 x 378
Lent from the Suida-Manning Collection

The story of how the Roman Senate's daring early defender, Gaius Mucius, earned his surname Scaevola, "the left-handed," has been treated by many artists from the time of the Renaissance onward. More than sixty versions are recorded in sculpture, paintings and prints, including works by Mantegna, Tintoretto, Guercino, Piazzetta, Rubens, Van Dyck, Poussin and Le Brun.[1]

It was a heroic subject and the young Boucher conceived it as a grandiose scene in the framework of baroque art. His sketch, containing no less than sixteen figures, was described as an "esquisse faite à Rome",[2] thus providing the clue to both the dating and the style of the composition. For it was during his student days in Italy (1727–1731) that Boucher absorbed some of the manner of the baroque artists whom he emulated in his youthful works, and it is this rather flamboyant quality which marks this drawing.

The tale of patriotism and civic virtue which Boucher chose to tell again concerned the inspiring feat of a Roman patrician who entered the enemy lines of the Etruscans, whose ruler Lars Porsenna was besieging the city. His attempt to kill the king failed, for his dagger struck the royal scribe by mistake, and Mucius was seized by the guards and brought before Lars Porsenna. "I am a Roman," he told the Etruscan ruler, "and I came here to kill you. I have as much courage to die as to kill. It is our Roman way to do and to suffer bravely."[3] Porsenna ordered the prisoner to be burnt alive, but Mucius thrust his right hand into the fire of the sacrificial altar and with incredible fortitude endured the pain of having it burnt off. "See how cheap men hold their bodies," he cried out, "when they care only for honor." Impressed by the young nobleman's heroic gesture, the Etruscan king granted him his liberty.

It is not clear whether the *"esquisse"* in the d'Orlemont Sale was an oil sketch or a preparatory, sketchy drawing in chalk; another drawing of the same subject, sold only a few years after Boucher's death, is specifically catalogued as "dessin à la pierre noire", and is also described as a "composition de 16 figures."[4]

This latter drawing sold in the Gros Sale (1778) might be a design for which the Suida-Manning drawing, also done in black chalk, could have served as a preliminary study, or else the latter sheet might actually have formed part of the Gros drawing, since the figures are abruptly cut off at the sides, and there might well have been a total of sixteen in the original composition.

1. Pigler, II, pp. 392-394.
2. According to Michel (no. 883), this sketch was sold with the collection of the Chevalier d'Orlemont in 1883.
3. Livy, bk. II ch. 12, trans. A. de Sélincourt, London, 1971.
4. Michel, no. 885.

3

Moses Receiving the Tablets of the Law

Pen, ink and bistre wash
400 x 292
Provenance: The artist (sale, Paris, Feb. 18, 1771, no. 393);
Anonymous sale, Paris, Apr. 1, 1776, no. 85; de Silvestre (sale,
Paris, Feb. 28-Mar. 25, 1811, no. 236); Vignère (sale, Paris,
Dec. 22, 1856, no. 11); Laperlier (sale, Paris, Feb. 17–18, 1879,
no. 62); Louis Silver
Bibliography: Goncourt, p. 188; Michel, p. 44, no. 808;
Ananoff, no. 681
Exhibited: Daniels Collection, 1968, no. 24, repr.
Lent by David Daniels

Boucher's biographer Pierre de Nolhac noted with some relief that after Boucher returned from Italy in 1731, he abandoned "the biography of Noah, Jacob and Gideon." Interestingly enough, it was during this period of the early 1730s, when he was completely under the spell of the Italian baroque, that Boucher chose to interpret a number of Old Testament themes. The stories of the Patriarchs, Abraham, Isaac and Jacob; Noah and the Ark; Ruth and Boaz; Samson and Delilah; Esther and Ahasuerus; Joseph and his brethren, all these gave the young artist a chance to match his virtuosity to the heroic exploits of Biblical heroes and heroines. With bold baroque sweep of pen and wash he created an image of the Creator: God the Father with arm upraised in awesome gesture, pointing to the Tablets of the Law on which are inscribed the Ten Commandments. The submissive figure of Moses, his face turned in reverence toward the divine presence, holds aloft the Tablets which bear the divine laws.

In the sale catalog of Boucher's effects, the drawing is listed as "Autre beau dessein, idem; hauteur 15 pouces, largeur 10

pouces 6 lignes; son sujet est Moyse qui reçoit les tables de la Loi des mains de Dieu, accompagné d'Anges." An anonymous sale which took place in Paris on April 1, 1776, lists the drawing as no. 85, "Dieu donnant les Tables de la Loi à Moïse, des Anges les environnent; ce dessein de *François Boucher* tient des Maîtres Italiens: il est à la plume et lavé; hauteur 15 pouces; largeur 11." Gabriel de Saint-Aubin attended this sale and made, in his catalog,[1] his usual notations and marginal illustrations which though minuscule, are perfectly legible. Opposite no. 85 he made a little sketch (one inch wide and two inches high) of Boucher's *Moses Receiving the Tablets of the Law.*

The *experts* who compiled the catalogs of important sales in the eighteenth century were the most knowledgeable men in the field of art: Mariette, Pierre Rémy, Julliot, Glomy. It is of special interest, therefore, to note the cataloger's comment, "ce dessein de François Boucher tient des Maîtres Italiens", for the drawing deliberately aims to achieve the effects of the Italian baroque.

1. Now in the collection of Mr. and Mrs. Charles Wrightsman.

Fig. 3. Castiglione. *Hagar and Ishmael.*
Drawing. Suida-Manning Collection

Hagar and Ishmael in the Desert

Black chalk on buff paper
297 x 216
Provenance: Rodrigues (Lugt 897)
Exhibited: Boucher, 1957, no. 7, pl. V; Iowa City, The
University of Iowa Museum of Art, "Drawing and the Human
Figure," 1964, no. 65. "1969 Fine Arts Festival
Exhibition," no. 18, repr.
Lent by The University of Iowa Museum of Art, Mark
Ranney Memorial Fund

Boucher's admiration for the work of the Genoese master Giovanni Benedetto Castiglione is well known: he painted pastoral *journeys* "dans le goût de Benedette," and collected paintings and drawings by him. The catalog of the Boucher Sale (Feb. 18, 1771) lists a painting by Castiglione (no. 3) and several drawings (nos. 210, 475). Of special interest is no. 210, *"Agar et Ismael, grand et beau dessein au pinceau,* par Jean Benoit Castiglione." This is almost certainly the drawing in the Suida-Manning Collection (fig. 3) of which several versions exist.[1] Boucher's drawing is so similar in its concept and compositional arrangement to Castiglione's vigorous brush drawing that one is tempted to see a close relationship between them.

The Suida-Manning drawing, *The Angel Appearing to Hagar in the Wilderness,* shows the seated figure of Hagar, her right arm outstretched in supplication toward the angel descending through the clouds, her left hand touching the child lying on the ground. In Boucher's drawing, Hagar, also seated, her supplicating face turned toward the angel, points to the objects at her side, the belongings which she took with her into the desert when she left Abraham's house. The sleeping infant Ishmael at her feet is turned away from her as if in utter exhaustion.

Are we justified in assuming that Boucher owned the Castiglione drawing from which his own composition is clearly derived—of which, in fact, it is almost a mirror image? Comparison between Castiglione's baroque treatment of the scene—Hagar's highly emotional gesture, the angel's draperies billowing in the air, cutting across the tree trunk, the suggestion of infinite space in the background—and Boucher's counter-clockwise rococo arrangement, set against a flat backdrop of trees; the calm tenderness which relates the figures to each other, emphasizes the lapse of a century which separates, for all their affinities, the French from the Genoese artist; the baroque from the rococo vision.

1. Cf. A. Percy, *Giovanni Benedetto Castiglione,* Philadelphia, 1971, p. 108, no. 82.

5
An Angel Feeding a Holy Hermit
Black chalk on buff paper
313 x 216
Glomy stamp G, lower right (Lugt 1119)
Provenance: The drawing was discovered in 1956 by Sir
Francis Watson in an album of prints and drawings in a
London salesroom, and came apparently from a private
English collection
Bibliography: K. M. Fenwick, "The Collection of Drawings,"
The National Gallery of Canada Bulletin, II, no. 2, 1964, pp.
2, 9, fig. 12; Popham and Fenwick, no. 221, p. 157, repr. p. 156;
Slatkin, 1967, p. 63; J. S. Boggs, *The National Gallery of
Canada,* London, 1971, no. 165, repr.
Exhibited: Boucher, 1957, no. 8, pl. VI; Slatkin, 1959, no. 43,
repr.; Toronto, Art Gallery of Ontario, "Master Drawings
from the Collection of the National Gallery of Canada," 1968,
no. 35, pl. 35; London, Colnaghi, "European Drawings from
the National Gallery of Canada, Ottawa," 1969, no. 44, fig.
44—also Paris (Louvre) and Florence (Uffizi, no. 34, pl. 34)
Lent by The National Gallery of Canada, Gift of Mrs. Samuel
Bronfman

Boucher's religious compositions present an enigma, for only
very few of the recorded paintings and drawings listed in
eighteenth century sales catalogs and identified on contemporary
engravings, appear to be extant, while a considerable number of
drawings based on Old and New Testament themes which are
undeniably by his hand, are unrecorded, unrelated to any painted
composition, and difficult to date.[1] There is, for instance, no
mention in contemporary records of Boucher's beautiful drawing
An Angel Feeding a Holy Hermit which is based on, or strongly
influenced by a Bolognese composition such as the drawing attributed to Cantarini in the Staedel Institut, Frankfurt, of an
angel appearing to St. Joseph (fig. 4). While the Ottawa drawing
is recognizably by Boucher's hand, it might have gone unnoticed,
had not his pupil Fragonard etched it—the only work by his
master he so recorded—and inscribed his plate: *Boucher invenit
et Delin. Fragonard Sculps.* (fig. 5).

1. It is interesting in this connection to find in the sales catalog of
Boucher's effects (1771) two copiously illustrated editions of Biblical subjects: *Figures du vieux et du Nouveau Testament en soixante-deux pièces
inventées et gravées par J. Luiken, belles épreuves* (no. 604) and *Histoire
du vieux et du nouveau Testament, par M. Basnage, avec figures de Romain
de Hoogue* (no. 605).

Fig. 4. Cantarini. *An Angel Appearing to St. Joseph.*
Drawing. Frankfurt, Städelsches Kunstinstitut

Fig. 5. Fragonard, after Boucher. *An Angel Feeding a Holy Hermit.* Etching. The Art Institute of Chicago, John H. Wrenn Memorial Collection

6

The Baptism of Christ

Pen, brown ink and wash over black chalk on cream paper
Oval, 256 x 199
Stamp of the mountmaker Glomy, bottom center: G (Lugt
1119). Inscribed in pencil, bottom left of mount: *par Boucher*
Provenance: The Hermitage
Bibliography: Slatkin, 1967, p. 63
Exhibited: Toronto, Ottawa, San Francisco, New York,
1972–73, no. 14, pl. 87
Lent by The St. Louis Art Museum

Although Boucher continued throughout his career to interpret
religious subjects, he gradually abandoned the Old Testament
themes which had enjoyed such popularity among the Bolognese
and Genoese artists of the seventeenth century. The *Bréviaire de
Paris* (1736) which Boucher illustrated, displayed three theologi-
cal Virtues and the figure of Religion, each dominating a view
of Paris: the Invalides, the Louvre, the Pont Neuf and Notre
Dame; the illustrations themselves were based on themes from
the New Testament. Henceforth he was to turn toward depicting
"les douces légendes Chrétiennes, le cycle que l'Eglise même
dénomme les mystères joyeux"; his style was to become less
flamboyant, adapting itself to themes of gentleness and compassion: the Nativity, the Adoration, the miracles and allegories
of the Faith.

Although *The Baptism of Christ* relates stylistically to *The
Holy Trinity,* a drawing which Boucher executed as a commission for Charles Rogers in 1765[1] (engraved by Watts[2] in 1771),
it was probably done in the 1730s when Boucher was still very
much under the influence of baroque Italy. Like *The Adoration*
in the Musée de Montpellier and *The Pilgrims of Emmaus in* The
Hermitage—all, incidentally, oval compositions—the *Baptism of
Christ* may have been intended as a project for an altarpiece
which was never executed.

1. Slatkin, 1967, p. 66, n. 57.
2. Incl. in C. Rogers, *A Collection of Prints in Imitation of Drawings,*
London, 1778, II, pl. after p. 198.

7

Christt and the Woman Taken in Adultery

Charcoal and gray wash heightened with white on gray paper
267 x 436
Bibliography: Slatkin, 1967, p. 63
Lent by The Metropolitan Museum of Art, Dodge Fund

Throughout his crowded career Boucher clung to the notion that he would some day paint an important religious composition. More than 200 recorded drawings and prints (many no longer extant), including illustrations for a breviary, designs for a series of engraved images of saints, and a number of devotional pictures, bear witness to his aspiration.

Boucher's models were the masters of the baroque whose work he had seen and admired as a young man in Italy, and whose prints and drawings he collected and studied after he returned to France. It was certainly a baroque master who inspired the painting, on a prescribed subject, which won the first prize at the Académie for Boucher, who was then twenty. *Evilmérodach, fils de Nebuchodonosor* (now in The Columbia Museum of Art, Samuel H. Kress Collection), done with great skill but little devout feeling, echoed the style of Luca Giordano and Solimena, and pointed the way toward achieving the coveted status of *peintre d'histoire sacré*. It was, however, an ambition which almost all of Boucher's patrons discouraged, and which his critics deplored. Diderot reserved his most scathing epithets for the religious paintings which Boucher exhibited at the Salon, rebuking him especially for his Madonnas which, said Diderot, were "worldly creatures in saintly disguise."

If the bravura of the baroque impressed the youthful artist, the dignity and nobility of the High Renaissance inspired him in his mature period; for it is surely to the Venetians of the sixteenth century that one must look for the prototype of the magnificent drawing *Christ and the Woman Taken in Adultery.* The friezelike aspect of the composition, the strict frontality of the principal figures, the classical overtones, strongly recall similar subjects by Titian. But the emotional impact of the pose and gestures are more reminiscent of Domenichino, whose frescoes Boucher had seen in the church attended by his com-

patriots in Rome—S. Luigi de' Francesi. Boucher never actually copied such paintings, as his pupil Fragonard was to do, but one cannot escape the feeling that the drawing in the Metropolitan Museum was inspired by an actual painting by a sixteenth century Venetian artist.

8

Four Heads of Cherubs

Black, red and white chalk on gray paper
319 x 252
Inscribed, lower left, in archaic script: *f. Boucher* with *paraphe*
Provenance: J. Pierpont Morgan (purchased from his estate)
Exhibited: New York, The Pierpont Morgan Library,
"Treasures from The Pierpont Morgan Library, Fiftieth
Anniversary Exhibition," 1957, no. 100; Hartford, Wadsworth
Atheneum, "The Pierpont Morgan Treasures," 1960, no. 82;
Stockholm, Nationalmuseum, "Pierpont Morgan Library
Gästar," 1970, no. 52.
Lent by The Pierpont Morgan Library

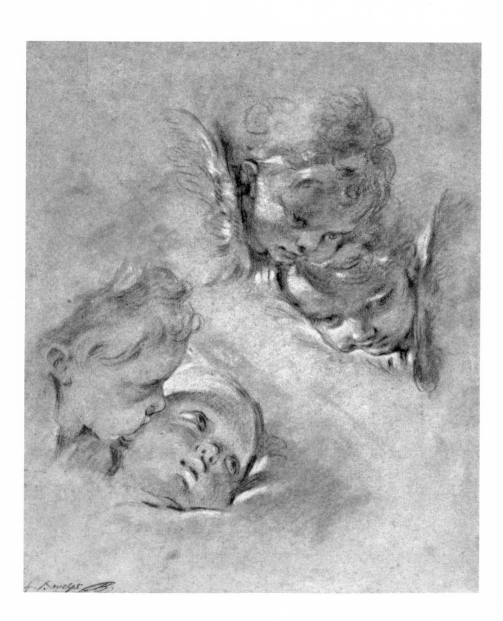

More than just a routine arrangement of *amoretti,* this drawing
of four infants' heads transformed into cherubs, each one recalling a study from life in other compositions, conveys the tender
feeling so frankly expressed in Boucher's studies of children.
Groups of cherubs appear in all his devotional pictures; one such
example is the *Madonna and Child* in the Metropolitan Museum,
where cherubs reinforce the image of innocence and purity of
the Christ Child and Infant St. John, which the artist strove to
convey.

Of particular interest is the inscription with its *paraphe* or
flourish which appears on this drawing, as well as on a number
of other drawings, all of unusually high quality. The inscription
f. Boucher with its use of the archaic letter *h* is not the artist's
signature. According to M. Babelon of the Archives Nationales,
Paris, it is an inscription affixed by a notary attesting the authenticity of drawings which formed part of an estate.

9
Two Children
Red chalk
223 x 215
Provenance: Charles Rogers (Lugt 624)
Lent anonymously

The English collector Charles Rogers owned several drawings
by Boucher, among them a *Virgin and Child* (Brinsley Ford Collection) and a *Holy Trinity*. These had been purchased for him,
according to Frits Lugt, by the engraver Robert Strange who had
spent some time in Paris studying with the printmaker Le Bas.
That Rogers should have included the drawing of two nude
children in his distinguished collection, along with works of a
more serious nature by the French master, is an indication of
the drawing's high quality and the pleasing nature of the subject.
Boucher's *sujets d'enfants* proved so popular that no less than five
Livres des groupes d'enfants were engraved, while individual
drawings of children were etched by Boucher himself and by
Madame de Pompadour.

Sleeping Infant
Black and white chalk on gray paper
214 X 200
Provenance: van Suchtelen (Lugt 2332); Weinmüller (sale, Munich, June 18, 1952)
Bibliography: The University of Michigan Museum of Art Bulletin, IV, 1969, p. 38
Lent by The University of Michigan Museum of Art

Fig. 6. *Halt at the Fountain* (detail).
Painting. Courtesy, Museum of Fine
Arts, Boston
Gift of the Heirs of Peter Parker

The Age of Reason was not particularly concerned with the world of children; yet many artists of the eighteenth century responded to the appeal of childhood, recording some of its phases with remarkable directness and intuitive understanding. The official portraits of noble and royal children, painted in all their grown-up finery, bedecked with plumes and decorations, staring vacantly at their silver rattles and elaborate toys were unable to capture the essence of childhood; Boucher's portrait of the two-year old Duc d'Orléans at Waddesdon comes to mind and the doll-like youngsters painted by Nattier, Drouais and Madame Vigée-Lebrun, with their pretty, expressionless faces. But Watteau was able to penetrate the secret world of children in his delightful drawings, which Boucher etched, and which doubtless inspired his own studies of children.

Boucher was clearly at home in this world, for children to him were not merely toy images to amuse adult society, nor were they symbols of *sensibilité*, but little creatures of flesh and blood. Can one doubt that the children whose likeness Boucher recorded with such humor and affection were those of his own household? They are sketched in those intimate moments of domestic life when children are caught off guard, having just fallen asleep, or just awakened, when they are being fed or held close, or reaching out for some enticing object. Such glimpses into the life of a child are afforded by many of Boucher's drawings: this *Sleeping Infant* and the same child, surely sketched within minutes while still sleeping soundly (Rijksmuseum), and again, seen from a different angle (Toronto, Markon Collection), and rubbing its eye before awakening (Boymans Museum). Boucher introduced this sleeping infant into a number of paintings of much later date, for example, the mother holding a child in her arms in the Boston Museum's *Halt at the Fountain* dated 1767 (fig. 6); the child first appeared in a painting on an Old Testament theme, *Le Départ de Jacob,* engraved by Elisabeth Cousinet, datable in the middle 1730s, when Boucher's own children were infants. A drawing in Stockholm of two sleeping children with a cat that has also dozed off was bought from Boucher by the Swedish ambassador, Count Tessin, but not before Boucher had made a delightful etching of it with the title *Le Sommeil.*

A Small Boy Drinking from a Bowl
Black chalk heightened with white on bluish-green paper
248 x 190
Inscribed on verso in eighteenth century hand: *Dessein
original de Boucher 24*
Provenance: Bertram
Lent anonymously

The subject of the little boy drinking from a bowl was a popular
one. A drawing in black chalk, heightened with white on blue
paper, entitled *Le Petit buveur de lait* (Michel, no. 2437) is
listed in the Roblin Sale (Feb. 17, 1905). This entry may refer
to our drawing, although the dimensions vary somewhat. A
biscuit de Sèvres by Falconet, *Enfants buvant du lait* (1759), was
probably based on an engraving by Daullé after a Boucher drawing *Les buveurs de lait* which shows two children, one of whom
closely resembles our little boy, drinking from a bowl.[1] The
little boy drinking his bowl of milk occurs again ten years later,
this time in a painting, *Idyllic Scene* (Walters Art Gallery, Baltimore) dated 1769.

1. Cf. C. Dauterman, *The Wrightsman Collection, IV, Porcelain,* New
York, 1970, no. 121, repr. p. 295.

12

Les Crêpes

Pen and brown wash
340 x 230
Provenance: Randon de Boisset (sale, Paris, Feb. 27, 1777, no. 342); Chevalier Lambert (sale, Paris, Mar. 27, 1787, no. 232); Marquess of Landsdowne; Lester F. Avnet
Bibliography: Michel, no. 1299
Exhibited: Slatkin, 1957, no. 20, repr. pl. XVIII Caracas, "Exposicion de Dibujos del Renacimiento al Siglo XX," 1957, no. 6; West Palm Beach, Norton Gallery and School of Art, "Old Master Drawings from the Collection of Mr. and Mrs. Lester Francis Avnet," Circulated by the American Federation of Arts, 1968, no. 5, repr.
Lent by Mr. and Mrs. Howard Weingrow

The influence of seventeenth century Holland, and more especially that of Rembrandt, is everywhere apparent in this striking drawing, with its brilliant use of wash. It recalls, once more, the fact that Boucher owned an important group of Rembrandt drawings which were sold with his effects in 1771. Randon de Boisset, whom Boucher advised in his purchases, and with whom he took a trip to the Low Countries in 1766, also showed a strong predilection for the Dutch School, and it is interesting that two of the drawings from the Randon de Boisset Collection in this exhibition, *Boy Holding a Carrot* (pl. 32) and *Les Crêpes* reflect the influence of Dutch art in Boucher's work.

13
Design for an Allegorical Dedication

Black chalk on buff paper
605 x 426
Inscribed, bottom center: *Cartel alegorique pour la justice*
Provenance: Léon Decloux
Exhibited: Boucher, 1957 (not in catalog)
Lent by the Cooper-Hewitt Museum of Decorative Arts and
Design, Smithsonian Institution

Owen McSwiny, an Irish impresario living in Venice in the
1720s, hit upon what he hoped would be a money-making
scheme: memorializing a number of Englishmen (famous and
dead) in a series of twenty-four paintings which would be
offered for sale to an interested milord as an important collection, for a handsome price. McSwiny commissioned a group of
well-known Italian artists, including Marco Ricci, G. B. Pittoni,
Canaletto, Creti and Piazzetta, to paint a series of splendid
allegorical tombs, honoring some of the outstanding heroes,
statesmen and scientists of Queen Anne's reign. Among
those immortalized in these monumental paintings were John
Churchill, Duke of Marlborough; Sidney Godolphin, the Lord
Treasurer; William Earl Cowper, the first Lord Chancellor;
Archbishop Tillotson; Charles Sackville; Sir Isaac Newton;
Robert Boyle; John Locke and Thomas Sydenham.

McSwiny's ambitious scheme did not meet with the success
he had hoped for, although he did manage to sell ten or eleven
paintings to the Duke of Richmond.[1] As an aid to selling the
original group of paintings McSwiny had decided to have an
expensively illustrated catalog of engravings published.[2] The
engraver's drawings (after the paintings by Marco Ricci, Pittoni,
etc.) were executed by D. M. Fratta; the engravings were by
various French engravers, including C. N. Cochin, D. Beauvais
and J. Ph. Le Bas. Boucher was commissioned to prepare eight
"half-titles" to accompany the engravings; Carle van Loo designed two more "half-titles;" all of these depicted in allegorical
terms the attributes, coats-of-arms and honorific titles of the
personalities memorialized in the twenty-four paintings of imaginary tombs.[3] The set of eight engravings which Boucher had
designed, with a frontispiece by Carle van Loo, was published
about 1736 as *Tombeaux des Princes, des Grands Capitaines et
autres Hommes illustres qui ont fleuri dans la Grande Bretagne
vers la fin du XVII et le commencement du XVIII Siècle. Gravés
Par les plus Habiles Maitres de Paris, d'après les Tableaux et
desseins originaux des plus célèbres Peintres d'Italie.* Carle van

Loo's design (engraved by Dorigny) of the Earl of Cadogan's memorial is dated 1736 on the engraved plate; Boucher's designs were probably done about the same time.[4] Some years later, Gabriel Huquier published the series of engraved "half-titles" in a reduced version.

The *Design for an Allegorical Dedication* in the Cooper-Hewitt Museum is Boucher's original drawing for the "half-title" to the engraved version by Beauvais of the memorial painting dedicated to William Earl Cowper, first Lord Chancellor. Before being appointed Lord Keeper of the Great Seal, Cowper had a distinguished legal career, which no doubt accounts for the inscription on the drawing: *Cartel alegorique pour la justice*.

Done with all the rococo inventiveness of the early thirties, when Boucher was closely associated with Juste-Aurèle Meissonier, this drawing echoes the *rocaille* style of the famous *ornemaniste*. The full repertory of allegorical allusions is here employed, with Fame, Wisdom and Honor personified by graceful female figures, and winged *amorini* surrounding the earl's coat-of-arms. The waving palm trees and billowing clouds appear frequently in Boucher's decorative designs of the thirties, for example, the frontispiece of the *Bréviaire de Paris* of 1736. Only two of Boucher's original drawings for the *Tombeaux des Princes* are known to have survived—the Cooper-Hewitt drawing and the design for the "half-title" to the allegorical tomb of William III of England. This latter drawing is in the collection of Sir Francis Watson.[5]

1. The remaining thirteen or fourteen were eventually sold off to a certain Sir William Morice, but painted copies and repetitions were also produced.

2. In a unique fly-sheet in The British Museum which, on internal evidence, can be dated around 1730, McSwiny announced his immediate intention of publishing the first eight engravings as a prelude to issuing engravings after all twenty-four tombs. The first set of engravings, according to Sir Francis Watson, must have appeared shortly after this date.

3. The "half-titles" were engraved by M. G. Aubert, D. Beauvais, Laurent Cars, Cochin the Younger, Duflos, Larmessin, Surugue and Tardieu. Most of these engravers also participated in the project of engraving the paintings of the tombs. However, only certain of the paintings had engraved "half titles."

4. Sir Francis Watson points out that the set of the *Tombeaux* engravings in The British Museum which formerly belonged to Consul Smith, McSwiny's contemporary, does have the date 1736 on the title page.

5. Much of the information for the above entry has been generously made available by Sir Francis Watson, Director of the Wallace Collection, who has made a thorough study of the pictures, their engraved versions, and the "half-titles" for which Boucher and Carle van Loo supplied the designs. For a fascinating account of McSwiney's undertaking see F. Haskell *Patrons and Painters,* London, 1963, pp. 287-292. One of the original paintings ordered by McSwiny, the *Memorial to Admiral Sir Clowdisley Shovell* by Sebastiano and Marco Ricci, is in the National Gallery of Art, Washington, Samuel H. Kress Collection.

14

Design for a Frontispiece: Love Staying the Hand of Time

Black chalk
606 x 408
Signed (inscribed?) lower right: *f. Boucher*
Exhibited: Boucher 1957, no. 2, repr.
Lent by The Metropolitan Museum of Art
Purchase, gift of Anne and Carl Stern

Stylistically related to Boucher's designs for the *Tombeaux des Princes* series, this drawing may either be a rejected design for the book's frontispiece (eventually executed by Carle van Loo) or for the pamphlet that was issued along with the series of engravings, or it may have been intended as a memorial for a famous literary figure. The open book supported by the figure of Fame with her trumpet, toward which one of the *amorini* is pointing; the book crowned with laurel and palm which lies at the foot of the cenotaph; Time with his scythe and hourglass, being fettered by the loves—all the allegorical vocabulary of the *Tombeaux* series—is here employed to sing the renown of a great poet or playwright such as John Dryden, for instance, whose play *All for Love* gained him lasting fame.

The dimensions of the drawing are almost the same as those of the two surviving designs, the Cooper-Hewitt sheet and that in the collection of Sir Francis Watson. The cartouche with its *rocaille* elements of curves and counter curves, even the curly foliage at the base of the monument are exactly those of the other *Tombeaux* designs. There can be little doubt that the drawing in the Metropolitan Museum is also part of this series, and that the date of 1736 can be assigned to it as well.

20

15

Design for an Overdoor Decoration

Black chalk on cream paper
153 x 217
Inscribed, bottom right on mount: *f Boucher*
Provenance: Edwin Bryant Crocker
Bibliography: Master Drawings from Sacramento, Sacramento,
1971, listed p. 148; P. Rosenberg, "Twenty French Drawings
in Sacramento," *Master Drawings, 8,* no. 1, 1970, p. 39
Exhibited: Sacramento, E. B. Crocker Art Gallery, "Drawings
of the Masters," 1959, no. 1
Lent by the E. B. Crocker Art Gallery

The elaborate decorative schemes in which Boucher participated,
such as the decorations of the Salle du Conseil at Fontainebleau,
the royal apartments at Versailles, the Hôtel de Soubise and the
various châteaux of Madame de Pompadour, called for designs
to fill spandrels, overdoors, wall compartments and ceilings, all
in the new, richly decorative rococo style. Possibly a design for
a stucco decoration in an elaborate interior, the figures of three
female nudes and a winged genie upholding a portrait, may have
been intended to memorialize a notable individual—an illustrious
ancestor, or perhaps the actual owner. Although Boucher's
designs for architectural decorations are surpassed in originality
by those of the outstanding painter-decorators Pineau, Lajoue
and his friend Juste-Aurèle Meissonier, they do display a lively
inventiveness and a nice sense of rhythmic balance in their use
of rococo ornament.

16

The Figures of Fame and Victory above an Arch

Black and white chalk on blue paper
196 x 349
Inscribed on verso by Portalis: *F. Boucher*
Provenance: Chennevières (Lugt 2073); Portalis (Lugt 2232); Charles Mewes
Lent by The Metropolitan Museum of Art, Rogers Fund

Boucher's inspiration for drawings of this kind may have been derived from a treatise current in his day, with engravings by two of his contemporaries: *Iconologie par Figures; ou, Traité complet des Allégories, Emblêmes etc . . . par M. M. Gravelot et Cochin.* This highly interesting iconology (undated, reprinted in 1972) was described as *Ouvrage utile aux Artistes, aux Amateurs et peuvent servir à l'éducation des jeunes personnes.* It was intended as a manual to define those "emblematic figures referred to by all the painters and sculptors of the period, and to include the interpretation and elucidation down to the last detail of the allegorical images forming the plastic and decorative expression common to artists."[1] There was little deviation from the models established for these allegorical figures—Fame blowing her trumpet, Victory bearing the laurel wreath, Time wielding his scythe—still, an artist of Boucher's versatility could achieve freshness and spontaneity in working these figures into architectural decorations. Since they were easily adaptable to the architecture of the period not only in France, but throughout Europe, Boucher's decorative designs enjoyed great popularity, especially through the medium of prints by Demarteau (*cf.* Leymarie, no. 231) and other engravers.

1. Minkoff reprint, Geneva, 1972, n.p.

17
Head of a Shepherd
Red chalk
176 x 142
Signed, lower left: *Boucher*
Lent by Mr. and Mrs. Bernard Lande

The peasants in Boucher's *pastorales* and the shepherds in his *Adorations* are usually idealized, done according to a formula derived from the drawing manuals then in use, like Bloemart's *Tekenboek*. There were exceptions, such as this *Head of a Shepherd*, which achieves a degree of realism uncommon in Boucher's work. The peculiar shape of the head, the wispy hair and beard, the look of resignation are not those of an idealized peasant, nor has the figure been invested with arcadian romance. The artist observed the shepherd in a moment of truth and set down his humble features with a compassion rarely found in the polished court art of the period.

18

Head of a Roman Soldier
Red, black and white chalk on buff paper
195 x 180
Glomy stamp (Lugt 1085), bottom right, under mat
Provenance: William Bourn; Filoli (sale, Woodside, Calif.,
Jan. 10, 1937); Mrs. Osgood Hooker, Sr., Osgood Hooker
Lent by the Achenbach Foundation for Graphic Arts,
California Palace of the Legion of Honor, Gift of
Osgood Hooker

One of Boucher's early works was a set of twelve drawings
engraved by Hutin with the title *Recueil de différents têtes
tirés de la colonne Trajane* (Michael, no. 2614). M. de Bailly, an
eighteenth century collector who owned a number of Boucher
drawings, had in his collection five studies of heads of soldiers
from Trajan's Column; these were all counterproofs of the
original drawings which Boucher had made after the sculptured heads. The de Bailly Sale catalog (Jan. 26, 1767, no. 59)
listed, in addition, *"le dessein d'une tête de soldat du même."*
Although no dimensions are given, comparison with Hutin's
prints make it clear that the *Head of a Roman Soldier* was either
the drawing in the de Bailly Collection or another of the original
drawings from the series.

19
Three Heads of Roman Soldiers
Black chalk heightened with white on buff paper
228 x 305
Lent by Michael Hall

This powerful drawing of three male heads is derived from the studies which Boucher made after the heads of Roman soldiers on Trajan's column. All three heads appear, in reverse, on the plates engraved by Hutin and discussed in the previous entry. The drawing, probably utilized by Boucher in one of his early religious works, represents three Roman soldiers, two of whom are wearing helmets; these are not the plumed helmets of officers, but the plain round helmets of the ordinary militia. Their faces express both fascination and horror, suggesting that they are watching an awesome spectacle inspiring these emotions. Such groups of soldiers are commonly found in scenes of the Passion such as *The Crucifixion* or *The Mocking of Christ,* and the drawing may well portray a group of Roman soldiers in such context done for a composition now lost. An engraving by Nathaniel Parr (act. 1742–51) of what, on the basis of stylistic evidence, must be considered a very early painting by Boucher, entitled *Jephthah's Rash Vow,* shows such groups of Roman soldiers wearing the same round helmets. Who is to say how many early works by Boucher based on Old and New Testament themes are still considered to be by other hands? If a sufficient number of drawings and prints dealing with religious subjects can be assembled, it may be possible to reconstruct a considerable proportion of his early work.

Fig. 7. *Aurora and Cephalus*.
Painting. Nancy, Musée des Beaux-Arts

20
Aurora
Red chalk heightened with white on buff paper
370 x 231
Signed, lower left: *f boucher*
Provenance: Peter Jones; Basil Dighton; Hon. Irwin Laughlin
Bibliography: Shoolman and Slatkin, no. 34, repr.; I.
Moskowitz and A. Mongan, *Great Drawings of All Time,*
New York, 1962, III, no. 694, repr.; Vallery-Radot, pl. 58
Exhibited: Washington, National Gallery of Art, 1967
Lent by Rear Admiral and Mrs. Hubert Chanler

In 1733 Boucher painted *Aurora and Cephalus* (Musée des Beaux-Arts, Nancy), perhaps the most dazzling of all his early works. It was the year he married the seventeen-year-old beauty, Jeanne Buseau, and it was undoubtedly she who served as the model for Aurora (fig. 7), for which this drawing is a study. Time and again Boucher's wife was to appear in his paintings during the 1730s and early forties, her features unaltered, her figure youthful and gracefully proportioned. Ten years after he painted her as Aurora, Boucher did a charming portrait of her, reclining on a *chaise longue* (Frick Collection).

The story of the dawn goddess Aurora abducting the beautiful youth Cephalus is told by Ovid:

> There on the top of flowering Hymettus
> Gold-haired Aurora, who dispelled night's shadows,
> Had caught me up and carried me away.[1]

But Cephalus was true to Procris whom he loved, and for this the jealous goddess punished him cruelly by causing him to kill Procris accidentally. Boucher again returned to this fable years later when he painted another version of *Aurora and Cephalus* (now in the Louvre), and when he did a drawing (engraved by Augustin de Saint-Aubin for Ovid's *Metamorphoses* published in a new translation by the Abbé Banier in 1767 (pl. 93).

One of the earliest studies of the female nude which Boucher was to draw and paint hundreds of times, this seated figure with its sense of palpable form and living structure, its subtle modeling and graceful, rhythmic contours, has hardly been surpassed in the artist's oeuvre.

1. Ovid, *The Metamorphoses.* New version by H. Gregory. New York, 1958, bk. VII, p. 196.

Fig. 8. Gabriel de Saint-Aubin.
Venus and Cupid.
Drawing in sale catalog
Mr. and Mrs. Charles Wrightsman
Collection

21

Venus and Cupid

Black chalk heightened with white and touches of blue chalk
on buff paper
287 x 177
Provenance: Anonymous sale, Paris, Apr. 1, 1776, no. 216;
van Suchtelen (Lugt 2332); Lord Spencer; Heseltine; Mary
Benjamin Rogers
Bibliography: Heseltine, 1913, no. 7, repr.; Ananoff, no. 780
Lent anonymously

The sculptural figure of Venus with its strongly modeled contours and body charged with immense vitality, yet retaining a measure of feminine grace, was exactly the sort of drawing that Boucher's patrons prized. It appeared in an anonymous eighteenth century sale which Gabriel de Saint-Aubin, that indefatigable reporter of Parisian life, attended, where it was catalogued as "Vénus & l'Amour, figures en pieds, dessinées à la mine de plomb, par F. Boucher, hauteur 6 pouces, largeur 4." (no. 83). The marginal illustration by Gabriel de Saint-Aubin (fig. 8) is a very accurate rendering of this *Venus and Cupid,* although it appears opposite an entry which refers to a painting by Boucher (no. 216). The catalog entries were certainly confused, for the title of the painting (no. 216), *Venus désarmant l'Amour,* undoubtedly refers to this drawing which shows Venus with Cupid's bow, gazing disapprovingly down at the little Cupid by her side, who carries on his shoulder his quiver of arrows. The sale catalog, now in the collection of Mr. and Mrs. Charles Wrightsman, contained a number of important works by Boucher, including two beautiful landscapes which the catalog notes as having been acquired directly from the artist. With so many entries, the error in the catalog is understandable. The same catalog also contains the drawing *Moses Receiving the Tablets of the Law* (pl. 3).

22

Lady Seated, Holding a Fan

Red chalk
236 x 180
Signed, lower right: *f. Boucher f*
Provenance: Marius Paulme (Lugt 1910; sale, Paris, May 13,
1929, no. 28, pl. 23)
Bibliography: François Boucher, Paris, Galerie Cailleux,
1964, disc. with no. 33
Exhibited: Boucher, 1932, no. 40; Oberlin, Allen Memorial
Art Museum, "Master Drawings of the 18th Century in
France and Italy," 1951, no. 2, pl. 2, in the Museum's *Bulletin,*
Winter 1951
Lent by Mr. and Mrs. Joseph Verner Reed

One of the lavishly illustrated books prepared for publication in the eighteenth century was an edition of the *Contes de La Fontaine,* planned by Nicolas de Larmessin Fils (1684–1755) to include thirty-eight plates after Lancret, Pater, Eisen, Vleughels, Le Clerc, and Boucher. Each artist contributed a number of drawings which were then engraved by a group of skilled engravers headed by Larmessin, who engraved twenty-three of the plates himself. Boucher illustrated four of the tales: *La Courtisane amoureuse, Le Calendrier des vieillards, Le Fleuve Scamandre,* and *Le Magnifique.* These *Contes* (not to be confused with the fables) were sophisticated tales, mainly derived from Boccaccio's *Decameron.*

Boucher illustrated them with the same grace and wit which had marked his drawings for the Molière edition three years earlier, dressing his worldly characters in the height of fashion placing them in elegantly furnished interiors. The lady holding a fan is a study for the wife of Aldobrandin in *Le Magnifique* (fig. 9), a tale of a jealous husband who was cuckolded by a wealthy Florentine known as *Le Magnifique.*

The edition of the *Contes de La Fontaine* for which Boucher did these illustrations was projected for publication in 1738,[1] which means that the drawings for the engraved illustrations were, necessarily, done somewhat earlier. One such drawing for the story, *La Courtisane amoureuse,* does exist and is, in fact, dated 1736 (James de Rothschild Collection, Waddesdon).[2] The same date should therefore be assigned to the *Lady Seated, Holding a Fan* in the Reed Collection, since this drawing, too, was a study for one of the illustrations for *Le Magnifique,* another of the La Fontaine stories.

Fig. 9. Larmessin, after Boucher.
Le Magnifique.
Etching-engraving. Washington,
National Gallery of Art
Widener Collection

Fig. 10. *Le Pique-nique.*
Painting. Private collection

The illustrations for the *Contes de La Fontaine* proved so successful that Larmessin issued them as a separate set, eventually selling the plates to Buldet who reissued them time and again. Boucher painted four little pictures of the four subjects he had illustrated; these are dated 1744 and 1745, some eight years after the original illustrations for the *Contes* were done.

Engravings were made after these paintings, as so often happened with popular works, but this common sequel must not obscure the unusual earlier sequence: drawing, engraved illustration, finally a painting based on the earlier versions,[3] and ultimately new engravings, after the painted subjects and derivative in quite a different way from the original La Fontaine illustrative engravings.

Misapprehension of this series of events has caused confusion, and accounts for the mistaken dating of a painting entitled *Le Pique-nique* (fig. 10) and all the studies for it as 1745, rather than eight years earlier. It is well to bear this in mind, so as to establish a logical sequence in Boucher's work. 1734, the year he was received at the Académie, saw the edition of the *Oeuvres de Molière* which he illustrated. In 1737 appeared his *Cris de Paris,* engraved by Ravenet and Le Bas, with figures that help, stylistically, to date his painting *Le Peintre à son Chevalet*[4] which we shall discuss further in connection with the drawing *Boy Holding a Portfolio of Sketches* (pl. 33). For the edition of the *Contes de La Fontaine* planned for 1738, Boucher prepared illustrations, for which the drawing in the Reed Collection is a study. It is the stylistic relationship of these "La Fontaine" drawings to the studies for *Le Pique-nique* including the *Seated Lady* in the Metropolitan Museum discussed in the next entry, which permits the dating of 1736/1738 for the latter drawing.

1. Lady Dilke (*French Engravers and Draughtsmen of the XVIII Century,* London, 1902, pp. 71, 97) twice refers to the 1738 edition of the *Contes de La Fontaine.* It should be noted, however, that she makes no comment which would not be consonant with her having seen only the suite of engravings originally commissioned as illustrations of the La Fontaine stories. This fact gains importance when it is discovered that no such actual text of La Fontaine is extant in either the Bibliothèque Nationale, The British Museum, or elsewhere. There is no evidence that the edition itself was ever published, although the suite of engraved illustrations was not only issued, but enjoyed great popularity. F. Courboin (*Histoire illustrée de la gravure en France,* Paris, 1924, II, pp. 48, 49 writes: "Larmessin . . . fils, qui fut un des graveurs du Cabinet Crozat, est surtout connu par la publication d'une série d'estampes sur les *Contes* de La Fontaine; il eut l'idée de publier, gravés dans le même format, une série de tableautins composés sur ce thème par Lancret, Pater, Boucher, Vleughels et Le Clerc; la série complète se compose de 38 pièces . . . quatre d'après Boucher. . ." One such suite, with title page, is in the Widener Collection at the National Gallery of Art, another was included in the recent Esmerian Sale (Paris, June 6, 1973, no. 48).
2. Repr. in Heseltine, 1913, no. 8.
3. See *François Boucher,* Paris, Galerie Cailleux, 1964, no. 29, repr.
4. Engraved by Igonet under the title *La Peinture.*

23
A Seated Lady

Red chalk
165 x 218
Provenance: H. Pannier; Alexandrine Sinsheimer
Lent by The Metropolitan Museum of Art, Bequest of
Alexandrine Sinsheimer

The *Seated Lady* in the Metropolitan Museum is a sketch for one of the figures in the painting *Le Pique-nique* in a French private collection (fig. 10). Like most of Boucher's elaborate compositions this painting is composed of groups for which there are individual studies, clearly from life, though probably posed in the studio. Among the elegant company picnicking in the woods is a young man who leans forward, his *tricorne* in hand, and offers refreshment to the couple seated on the grass; the Musée des Beaux-Arts, Orléans, owns a drawing in red chalk which is a study for this young man (fig. 11). Another red chalk drawing of the valet carrying a platter of food, at the extreme right, is in a French private collection (fig. 12). Other figures in the painting are also recognizable in the Orléans study sheet, although their relation to each other and to the group as a whole has been altered. A drawing in a private English collection for the lady holding a cup immediately behind the *Seated Lady* is, incidentally, signed with the same signature as the drawing in Orléans, and the *Valet*.

The Metropolitan Museum's *Seated Lady,* who, in the painting, is coquettishly flirting with the gallant reposing at her feet, is one of the central figures in this delightful gathering. Often confused with this sheet is the Reed drawing (pl. 22) datable 1736/38; although it is likely that both figures were sketched from the same model, and within a short space of time, their costumes, worked out in precise detail, are quite different. The relationship between these two studies is of particular interest in regard to the date of *Le Pique-nique,* previously dated c.1745/47, and the various drawings for it.

Fig. 11. *Young Man, with Figures in Background.*
Drawing. Orléans, Musée des Beaux-Arts

Fig. 12. *A Valet.*
Drawing. France, private collection

24
Seated Male Nude

Red chalk on buff paper
495 x 395
Signed and dated, lower right: *J. Boucher 1738*. Inscribed,
lower left, with the inventory number of the *Académie
Royale de Peinture et Sculpture: Acad. Roy. N. XII*
Provenance: Académie Royale de Peinture et Sculpture,
Paris
Bibliography: Slatkin, 1967, p. 56, pl. 47
Lent by Norbert L. H. Roesler

On July 7, 1737, Boucher was appointed *professeur titulaire* at
the Académie Royale where for the next thirty years he taught
painting and drawing, attaining, in 1765, the directorship of the
Académie. Many of his studies of nudes were done for the
benefit of the students from models who posed in class; subsequently, groups of these *académies* were engraved and published as *recueils* by various printmaking establishments in Paris.
Boucher himself etched two of his *académies d'homme*, and
Louis Félix de La Rue etched twelve of Boucher's male nudes in
his *Livre D'Académies dessines d'Après le naturel Par François.
Boucher Peintre du Roy*. The *Seated Male Nude* in the Roesler
Collection was done the year after Boucher became professor
at the Académie. Although the drawings done by the teaching
staff were Crown property, some of them were apparently dispersed at some point; like the *Seated Male Nude,* they are
inscribed with the inventory number of the Académie. The
model who posed for this handsome drawing is familiar from a
number of paintings which Boucher did in the late thirties.

25
Seated Male Nude

Red chalk on buff paper
464 x 323
Inscribed, lower right, in an eighteenth century hand:
Boucher
Provenance: H. Michel-Levy (sale, Paris, May 12–13, 1919,
no. 55); Archibald Russell (Lugt 2770a; sale, London,
Sotheby, May 22, 1928, no. 97, as *Vulcan*)
Bibliography: Ananoff, no. 531
Exhibited: "Boucher," 1957, no. 25, pl. XXIII
Lent by Mr. and Mrs. Gerald Bronfman

The solid modeling and strong outline which define the form
of this male nude relate the drawing to the series of *académies
d'homme* which Boucher did while he was teaching at the
Académie Royale in the 1730s and forties. Although not connected with any specific figure in a painting, this vigorous male
nude might well have served as a study for *Vulcan* in one of
Boucher's mythological compositions.

26

Two Male Nudes

Red chalk
460 x 330

Provenance: Probably Sireuil (1781); Olivier (Lugt, Suppl., 1373)

Exhibited: Iowa City, University of Iowa, 1964, "Drawing and the Human Figure," no. 68. repr.

Lent by David Daniels

This powerful drawing of two male nudes was perhaps intended as a study for a painted composition, such as the struggle between Hercules and Anteus, rather than merely another *académie d'homme*. As far as can be determined, Boucher did not utilize it in any painting, nor was it engraved. According to Lugt, it was acquired, along with an important group of old master drawings by the English collector, Colonel Henry Stephen Olivier, in Paris about the middle of the nineteenth century. It is, in all likelihood, the drawing listed in the Sireuil catalog (1781) as no. 212: *Deux Lutteurs. Groupe d' Académie au crayon rouge. Hauteur 15 pouces, largeur 18 pouces.* The measurements in the Sireuil catalog are reversed but correspond closely to those of the Daniels drawing.

27
A Warrior

Black chalk heightened with white chalk
395 x 265
Signed, lower left: *f. boucher*. Stamp of the mountmaker
Glomy, lower right (Lugt 1119)
Provenance: Jean Dubois (sale, Paris, Mar. 21–22, 1927, no. 3,
repr.)
Bibliography: Ananoff, no. 992; Jean-Richard, p. 39
Exhibited: Boucher, 1932, no. 39; Boucher, 1957, no. 10
Lent by the Museum of Art, Rhode Island School of Design

Fig. 13. *A Warrior.*
Etching. Paris, Musée du Louvre,
Rothschild Collection

One of a series of studies of warriors in antique costume which
Boucher introduced in his paintings of Vulcan's Forge, done in
the late forties. Boucher etched this drawing himself;[1] it was
published as plate 3 in his *Nouveau livre de diverses figures
inventées et gravées en partie par François Boucher peintre du
Roy, à Paris chez Huquier.* The etching (fig. 13) is signed and
dated 1751 in the plate, but the drawing may have been done
earlier.

1. Baudicour, II, p. 43, no. 8.

36

28

Venus Reclining against a Dolphin
Black chalk heightened with white on buff paper
228 x 343
Provenance: Countess Sala (sale, New York, Parke-Bernet,
Nov. 18, 1961, no. 179); Louis Silver; Norton Simon (sale,
New York, Parke-Bernet, May 7, 1971, no. 206)
Bibliography: Slatkin, 1972, pp. 276–278, pl. 38
Exhibited: Oklahoma City, Oklahoma Art Center,
"The Armand Hammer Collection," 1971, no. 68, repr.; also at
Fine Arts Gallery of San Diego; Los Angeles County Museum;
London, Royal Academy of Arts, 1972; Dublin, National
Gallery of Ireland; Leningrad, The Hermitage; Moscow,
Pushkin Museum, 1972–73; Kiev, State Museum of Fine Art
of the Ukraine Soviet Socialist Republic, 1973
Lent by The Armand Hammer Foundation

This drawing of Boucher's favorite subject, the *Reclining Venus,*
while done with great delicacy, is not, as has been suggested,[1]
a counterproof. Comparison with other versions, which are
clearly copies, indicates that the Hammer drawing is the original
drawing by Boucher, engraved by Demarteau c.1746. (Leymarie,
no. 88), and dedicated to his friend, the painter Peyrotte.[2] The
drawing was also used as the basis for a painting (whereabouts
unknown) which J. C. le Vasseur engraved after Boucher had
been made *Premier Peintre du roi* and director of the Académie
Royale in 1765. The nymph in the painting is based on a drawing
in the Cabinet des Dessins of the Louvre; three putti and a
triton complete the composition.

1. *The Armand Hammer Collection,* Los Angeles, 1971, no. 68.
2. Slatkin, 1972, pp. 276-278.

Fig. 14. Huquier, after Boucher.
The Fountain.
Etching-engraving. Washington,
National Gallery of Art
Rosenwald Collection

29
The Fountain

Black and reddish-brown chalk heightened with white chalk
on buff paper
381 x 223
Inscribed, lower left: *Boucher*
Provenance: Franz Lederer; Erich Lederer
Exhibited: Minneapolis, University of Minnesota, "The
Eighteenth Century," 1961 no. 6, pl. 1; Toronto, Ottawa,
San Francisco, New York, 1972–73, no. 12, pl. 85
Lent by The Cleveland Museum of Art, John L. Severance
Fund

Gabriel Huquier etched this rococo fountain design in reverse,
as part of the first *Recueil* he published. Although the engraver's
version often falls short of the artist's original concept, Huquier's
etching (fig. 14) infuses a routine design with the restless,
dynamic quality peculiar to *rocaille* ornament. "Huquier modi-
fied the drawing considerably," wrote Hylton Thomas; "the
rocky background became a rustic niche with plants; the flow of
water was emphasized and systematized; *staffage* elements in
the foreground and at the sides were noticeably expanded."[1]

The dating of Boucher's fountain designs is generally established by the announcements of the engraved *Recueils* which
appeared in the *Mercure de France*. "The fountains of a suite
engraved by Huquier, datable by the *Mercure* of April 1736, are
richly sculptural, with shell basins irregularly composed, as are
the frames of certain more purely ornamental compositions committed to copper by the same engraver."[2]

Basically relying on the decorative scheme of Watteau's arabes-
ques, fascinated by the rococo inventions of Juste-Aurèle Meissonier, Boucher nevertheless managed to add his own elegant,
imaginative and distinctly personal note to the designs for the
Recueils des Fontaines.

1. *The Eighteenth Century,* exhibition catalog notes by H. Thomas,
Minneapolis, 1961, p. 18.
2. F. Kimball, *The Creation of the Rococo,* Philadelphia, 1943, p. 173.

30
Design for a Fountain

Black and white chalk on blue paper
191 x 261
Exhibited: Lawrence, University of Kansas Museum of Art,
"Fontinalia: the art of the fountain and the fountain in art,"
1957, no. 46, repr. p. 7; New York, Knoedler, "Great Master
Drawings of Seven Centuries," 1959, no. 53, pl. 50
Lent by The St. Louis Art Museum

Although fountains did not play the same dramatic role in the planning of French towns as in Bernini's Rome, a tradition of fountain design reaching back to the court of François I at Fontainebleau was still very much alive in France. Many books on the designing of fountains were published; among these was the *Receuil (sic) de Fontaines Inventées par F. Boucher,* engraved by Gabriel Huquier the Elder (1695–1772), who was a publisher as well as a printseller. This collection contained seven fountain designs in the lively rococo style which made use of asymmetric curves and countercurves, creating an effect of airiness and graceful elegance.

Predominant in the first quarter of the eighteenth century, the *rocaille* style was still much in vogue in the 1730s when Boucher and other artists of his day used its highly decorative idiom to invent new forms in vases, frames, screens and fountains. The St. Louis drawing, of two graceful water nymphs with infant tritons supporting a basin into which water flows from an urn, was probably not intended as a design for an actual fountain to be constructed; Boucher liked to imagine fountains set, quite improbably, at the edge of a forest, or beside a millstream, in the background of his pastoral paintings. There, beneath the rococo fountains, dolphins frolicked and nymphs displayed their languid charms against lush foliage and pearly conch shells.

The *Design for a Fountain* from St. Louis, for which no known engraving exists, is almost classic in feeling by comparison with the Cleveland fountain design (pl. 29); the former, an evenly balanced composition, recalls an antique bas-relief. As Edward A. Maser wrote, "Continuing the Baroque tradition, the age of Rococo also produced great fountains, but usually more intimate and elegant ones, which emphasized the gentle and graceful interplay of water and sculpture. The spectacular effects sought during the previous century are replaced by an appreciation of quiet and mildly moving water, not necessarily intricately combined with sculpture, but complementing it harmoniously, amid more calculatedly 'natural' settings." [1]

1. *Fontinalia: the art of the fountain and the fountain in art,* catalog notes by E. A. Maser, Lawrence, 1957, p. 25.

31
Triton and Naiad

Black and white chalk on gray paper
242 X 407
Bibliography: P. Mantz, *Boucher, Lemoine et Natoire,* Paris, 1880, p. 148, repr.
Exhibited: London, Savile Gallery, "Drawings by Old Masters," 1929, no. 15, repr., as by J. H. Taraval; Providence, Rhode Island School of Design, 1931; Cambridge, Fogg Art Museum, "French Drawings and Prints of the Nineteenth Century," 1934, no. 3; Buffalo, Albright Art Gallery, "Master Drawings," 1935, no. 68, repr. pl. 68; San Francisco, 1940, no. 8; Omaha, Joslyn Art Museum, 1941–1946; Oberlin, Allen Memorial Art Museum, "Master Drawings of the 18th Century in France and Italy," 1951, no. 1, pl. 1 in the museum's *Bulletin,* Winter 1951; Palm Beach, Society of the Four Arts, 1952–53; London, Royal Academy of Arts, "European Masters of the Eighteenth Century," 1954–55, no. 425
Lent anonymously

Nymphs abducted by tritons are the *staffage* figures in Boucher's mythological compositions based on such themes as the Birth and Triumph of Venus, the Triumph of Amphitrite, Neptune and Amymone, where sea monsters and dolphins are tossed about in wild abandon on the turbulent waves. The group of a triton blowing his conch shell as though announcing the graceful prize he had just captured, does not, as far as can be ascertained, form part of any known painting.

32
Boy Holding a Carrot

Pastel
306 x 242
Signed and dated, upper left: *f. Boucher 1738*
Provenance: Dézallier d'Argenville (sale, Paris, 1766, no. 72);
Randon de Boisset (sale, Paris, Feb. 27, 1777, no. 201);
Bruun-Neergard (sale, Paris, Aug. 30, 1814, no. 45);
Anonymous sale, Paris, Dec. 7, 1970, no. 1, repr.
Bibliography: Goncourt, p. 201; Michel, p. 41, no. 2395;
The Art Institute of Chicago Annual Report 1970–1971, p. 12,
repr. in color on the cover
Lent by the Art Institute of Chicago, The Joseph and Helen
Regenstein Collection

Boucher's interest in portraiture was limited. Apart from his noble patrons—Madame de Pompadour, Madame de Bergeret, the Marquis de Marigny, the Maréchal de Lowendal, the king and the children of the royal household—as well as members of his own family, he did not attempt to compete with his colleagues Portail, Drouais or de La Tour in painting the reigning beauties, and he left to Lundberg and Roslin the important personalities of his day. The *Boy Holding a Carrot,* an exception in Boucher's œuvre, is interesting for its fresh and intimate portrayal of the young lad, clearly a study from life, highly individualized, and for its connection with seventeenth century Dutch still life painting which Boucher held in high regard.

In the Dézallier d'Argenville and Randon de Boisset catalogs, the boy is described as holding a carrot, while the Brunn-Neergard catalog describes the vegetable as *"un panais"*, a parsnip. In the interest of botanical accuracy it must be stated that the vegetable could be either, since the parsnip is a member of the carrot family, and a species of white carrot was, according to Larousse, used for cattle fodder. Whatever the vegetable, the same lad is seen holding one in each hand, in a study sheet in red chalk which Boucher must have sketched from life (fig. 15). In this sheet,[1] the head and shoulders of the boy, who may have been a studio apprentice, appear at right, his bare, crossed legs in a reclining position at left, and at the bottom, the two hands holding the carrot.

The figure of the boy is to be seen again in one of Boucher's early paintings, the *Pastorale* from the Walter P. Chrysler Collection (fig. 16), for which the study sheet mentioned above is a preparatory drawing. Here he appears as a farm boy, offering his bountiful produce to the lady holding a huge head of cabbage.

A drawing, in the Ten Cate Collection (fig. 17) is also a study for an early painting—the *Pastorale* (formerly Rodolphe Kann Collection)[2]—which shows the boy once more, again with a bunch of carrots.

He must have been a good model, this winsome lad, for Boucher uses him, in exactly the same pose as in the Chicago pastel, in another early picture of great charm, the *Kitchen-Maid and Young Boy* (fig. 17A). Here he is seen beguiling a young woman with his smile and an offer of fresh vegetables, holding out his customary carrot. The theme and style of this painting are frankly derived from the Dutch *petits maîtres*, and since the pastel portrait of the boy (pl. 32) is dated 1738, it becomes evident that the Dutch influence continued to be strongly felt in Boucher's work throughout the thirties. It may be said that the pastel *Boy Holding a Carrot* shows Boucher's style, which had already approached full maturity, still marked by the vigor of Dutch realism, summing up whatever he had learned from Dutch genre. But the care which he bestowed in portraying the dimple-cheeked, curly-haired lad, dressed, not as the peasant boy of the early paintings, but in elegant city clothes, announces the suave manner of the court painter's style of the forties and fifties.

1. *Feuille d'études,* Léon Michel-Lévy sale, Paris, June 17, 1925, no. 33, repr.

2. Repr., *Catalogue of the Rodolphe Kann Collection,* Paris, 1907, II, pl. 145.

Fig. 15. *Sheet of Studies.*
Drawing. Formerly Michel-Lévy
Collection

Fig. 16. *Pastorale* (detail).
Painting. Chrysler Museum of
Norfolk

Fig. 17. *Boy, on Ground, Holding
Carrot.*
Drawing. Ten Cate Collection

Fig. 17A. *Kitchen-Maid and Young
Boy.*
Painting. Paris, private collection

33
Boy Holding a Portfolio of Sketches

Red, black and white chalk on buff paper
219 x 152
Collector's mark, *EC*, lower right
Provenance: Louis-Antoine-Auguste Rohan-Chabot (sale,
Paris, Dec. 8, 1807, no. 31); Utterson; Heseltine; Mary
Benjamin Rogers
Bibliography: Heseltine, 1900, no. 1, as by Watteau, repr.;
Heseltine, 1913, no. 100, as by Watteau, repr.; A. Ananoff,
"Un dessin de Boucher," *Bulletin de la Société de l'Histoire
de l'Art français,* Oct. 16, 1965; Ananoff, no. 545, fig. 102;
Apollo, p. 284
Lent anonymously

It is easy to see why this drawing of the youth in the *tricorne*
should have been attributed to Watteau; like Boucher's self-
portrait as a young man (pl. 1), it recalls Watteau's manner of
drawing, casual, yet precise, freely sketched but incisive. Yet the
hand is without question Boucher's and not Watteau's, for as
in the little self-portrait there is a new element of characterization
in the face and a high degree of individuation which marks it
off sharply from similar studies by Watteau.

The suggestion that the young boy who also appears at the
right of the easel in Boucher's painting *Le Peintre à son chevalet*[1]
is the youthful Deshayes who became Boucher's son-in-law, is
not tenable,[2] for Deshayes was born in 1729, and there is good
reason to believe that the painting was done about 1736 or perhaps a year or two later when Deshayes would have been no
more than seven or eight years old. But the youth in the drawing
is at least fourteen. Perhaps he was an apprentice who also
served as a model, in Boucher's studio, for Boucher did another
drawing of him (Mr. and Mrs. Bernard Lande Collection), a
direct portrait study which shows him at about the same age.
In the painting *Le Peintre à son chevalet* Bouche used him as
a *staffage* figure, to round out the composition, but then he is
a little urchin, running about the studio barefoot, and it is doubt-
ful that Boucher would have so portrayed his young pupil.

1. Engraved by Igonet in 1752, with the title *La Peinture.*
2. See *Apollo,* p. 284.

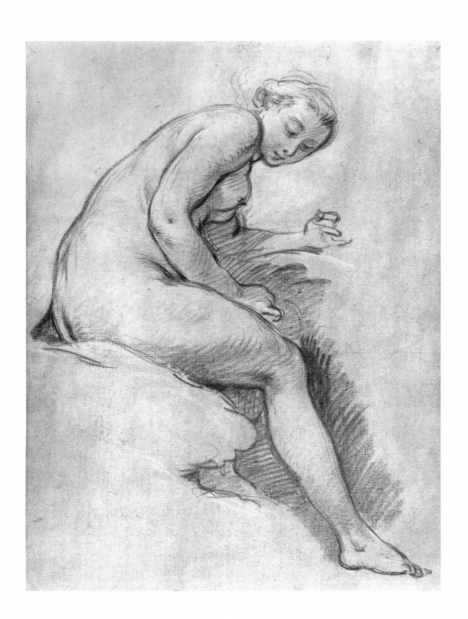

34
Seated Female Nude

Red chalk
287 x 210
Provenance: Lanna; J. Paul Richter [?] (sale, Amsterdam,
May 27–28, 1913, no. 273, pl. 38)
Bibliography: Gallery Notes, The Buffalo Fine Arts Academy,
1954, *18,* no. 3, cat. no. 59, fig. 6
Exhibited: Boucher, 1957, no. 16; Iowa City, University of
Iowa Museum of Art, "Drawing and the Human Figure,
1400–1964," 1964, no. 67
Lent by the Albright-Knox Art Gallery, Charlotte A. Watson
Fund

In the Salon of 1738 Boucher exhibited a painting, *The Three
Graces,* intended for the bedchamber of the Princesse de Soubise,
in the newly rebuilt and refurbished Hôtel de Soubise. This magnificent building (now the Archives Nationales in the rue des
Francs-Bourgeois) is one of the few remaining eighteenth
century palaces where Boucher's paintings can still be seen *in situ,*
in the very location for which they were designed. These dazzling decorations earned for Boucher, early in his career, the
reputation of *habile décorateur.* He had, by then, been appointed
professor at the Académie Royale where he made innumerable
drawings of nudes as teaching material for his students. The
Académie provided only male models, the female models posing
in the artist's studio.

The *Seated Female Nude,* exquisitely drawn in red chalk, may
have been done with the eventual composition of the *Three
Graces* in mind, as would seem to be indicated by the position
of the left hand which, in the painting, holds a flower; it may
also have been a study from life, posed in the studio and utilized
as one of the components of an ensemble. Another, identical
version of the Hôtel de Soubise painting is in the Gulbenkian
Foundation, Lisbon.

35
Reclining Female Nude

Red chalk heightened with white on gray-brown paper
315 x 415
Signed in ink near the lower margin: *fr. Boucher*
Provenance: Alphonse Kann (sale, Paris, Dec. 6–8, 1920, no.
74, repr.); John Nicholas Brown; Paul J. Sachs
Bibliography: Fogg Museum Notes, Cambridge, 1931, p. 316;
A. Mongan and P. Sachs, *Drawings in the Fogg Museum of
Art,* Cambridge, 1940, I, no. 596, p. 319, II, fig. 305; W. G.
Constable, "The Nude: Showing a Five-Century Ideal," *Art
News,* Jan. 15, 1946, repr. p. 10; Sachs, P., *The Pocket Book
of Great Drawings,* New York, 1951, pp. 88–90, repr. color,
inside back cover, Los Angeles County Museum, *Catalogue of
Paintings,* 1954, I, p. 63, repr. p. 62
Exhibited: Hartford, Wadsworth Atheneum, "The Nude in
Art," 1946, no. 6; Andover, Addison Gallery, 1946–1947; New
York, Century Club, "French Drawings from the Fogg Art
Museum," 1947; Richmond, Virginia Museum of Fine Arts,
1952; Waterville, Maine, Colby College, "Drawings," 1952,
no. 10; Boucher, 1957, no. 4, pl. 2; Paris, Orangerie, 1958, no.
32, pl. 42; Cambridge, Fogg Art Museum, "Works of Art
from the Collection of Paul J. Sachs," 1965–66, no. 29, repr.,
also New York, Museum of Modern Art, 1966–67
Lent by the Fogg Art Museum, Harvard University,
Bequest of Meta and Paul Sachs

Among the commissions which Boucher executed in the late
thirties were the decorations for the princely Hôtel de Soubise
and the town house of the Comte de Langonnay in the fashionable rue de Varenne, on the Left Bank. Two paintings from
this elegant mansion, *Venus and Mars* and *Venus and Mercury
Instructing Cupid,* designed as overdoor decorations, are now
in the Los Angeles County Museum. The *Reclining Nude* is
a study for the Venus in the latter composition (fig. 18) which
bears the date 1738. Quite possibly also a life study, the *Reclining
Nude* is an excellent illustration of a tour de force which is
peculiarly Boucher's own: turning a female nude into a decorative arabesque.

Fig. 18. *Venus and Mercury
Instructing Cupid.*
Painting. Los Angeles County Museum
William Randolph Hearst Collection

36

A Valet Serving Chocolate

Red and black chalk heightened with white over pencil on buff paper

345 x 195

Provenance: Norblin de la Gourdaine; Baronne de Connantré; Baronne de Ruble; Madame de Witte; Marquise de Bryas

Bibliography: Goncourt, p. 199; Michel, no. 1279; Vallery-Radot, pl. 54; Carlson, p. 158, pl. 21; Slatkin, 1967, p. 63

Exhibited: Wildenstein, 1963, no. 47

Lent by The Art Institute of Chicago, The Joseph and Helen Regenstein Collection

In 1739 Boucher painted *Le Déjeuner,* a delightful family scene in a handsome interior, with two ladies and two small children being served by a valet (fig. 19). The painting, now in the Louvre, is believed to represent Boucher's family,[1] his wife, who was then about twenty-six, and his two eldest children. His daughter Jeanne-Elisabeth-Victoire, was then about four and his son, Juste-Nathan, a year younger. The valet serving chocolate from a silver pot (surely not coffee, though the drawing was once known as *Le Cafetier*[2] is shown in full-length in the drawing, suggesting a life study from a studio model; in the painting his figure is partly hidden.

Two studies exist for the lady at the right, presumably Madame Boucher: a drawing in the same medium as the *Valet,* red and black chalk heightened with white is in The Hermitage; another (inscribed *Chardin*) is in the collection of Prince Liechtenstein.[3] Both these drawings, done with great delicacy and precision, form a striking contrast to the vigorous draftsmanship of the *Valet.*

Probably derived from and certainly influenced by Boucher's *Valet* is a similar figure in the painting *La Tasse de chocolat* by Nicolas Lancret (1690–1743).[4] Lancret, whom Michael Levey perceptively describes as "nearer Boucher than Watteau", painted *La Tasse de chocolat* in 1742, the year before he died and three years after Boucher's picture was painted. Lancret's family group is being served in a delightful garden; Boucher's is seated in an elegantly furnished room, but only the setting differs—the scene is clearly the same, and the figures of the two valets are closely related.

1. J. Cailleux, *François Boucher,* Paris 1964, no. 17, writes: "On reconnaît dans cette peinture Madame Boucher, alors âgée de vingt-six ans, avec ses deux premiers enfants: Jeanne-Elisabeth-Victoire, née en 1735, et Juste-Nathan, né en 1736. L'intérieur doit être celui où Boucher vivait alors, rue Saint-Thomas-du Louvre."

2. The engraving which Lépicié did of the painting *Le Déjeuner* does assume that the beverage is coffee, for the quatrain reads:

> *Caffé charmant ta liqueur agréable*
> *De Bacchus calme les accès*
> *Ton feu divin dissipe de la table*
> *Et les dégoûts et les excès.*

That coffee dissipates a hangover is no reason why it should be served to little children at the breakfast table; no doubt the printmaker devised his quatrain to make the print more saleable. As for the etching which the German engraver F. Hillemacher produced in 1857, entitled *Un caffetier (sic) de Paris en 1754,* it renders Boucher's drawings in a coarse and fumbling manner and confounds confusion by assigning a wrong title as well as a wrong date to the original drawing.

3. J. Schönbrunner and J. Meder, *Handzeichnungen alter Meister aus der Albertina und anderen Sammlungen,* Vienna, II, 1897, no. 131, repr. as by Chardin. The Hermitage drawing is also reproduced in the Hermitage catalog of the Boucher exhibition of 1970, no. 17.

4. Repr., Levey, pl. 19.

Fig. 19. *Le Déjeuner.*
Painting. Paris, Musée du Louvre

37
Hebe

Red and black chalk with wash, heightened with white, on
gray paper
341 x 225
Provenance: Anonymous sale, Paris, Apr. 14–15, 1845, no. 49;
L. Coblentz (sale, Paris, Jan. 24–25, 1917, no. 25, pl. 1);
Anonymous sale, Paris, Nov. 22, 1920, no. 4
Bibliography: Ananoff, no. 747, fig. 122
Lent anonymously

The sculptural quality of the richly draped figure of Hebe suggests the drawing might have been a design for a Sèvres model
or perhaps for one of the statues in the gardens of Versailles or
Madame de Pompadour's château at Crécy or Bellevue. The
figure actually occurs in a tapestry which Boucher designed for
the Beauvais looms in 1739 *(Psyche Displaying Her Treasures).*[1]
Here she is the nymph standing beneath an urn, making the
same gesture with both arms upraised. Some ten years later she
appears, even more precisely, as the nymph holding cymbals in
another tapestry, *Jupiter en Raisin* from *The Loves of the Gods*
series.[2] The drawing may also be connected with Rameau's
opera-ballet *Les fêtes d'Hébé* performed in 1739, as Boucher was
associated with Rameau in the production of several operas,
including *Les Indes galantes, Castor and Pollux* and *Pygmalion,*
for which he designed the sets and costumes.

1. Repr. by Badin, opposite p. 52.
2. See Badin, p. 61. The tapestry is repr. on the right of pl. 241 in the
Polovtsoff Sale catalog (Paris, Dec. 2-4, 1909), where it is combined with
the *Ariadne and Bacchus* tapestry.

38

Zephyr Leading Psyche into the Palace of Love
Black and white chalk on buff paper
310 x 270
Bibliography: Jean-Richard, p. 89, no. 90
Exhibited: Boucher, 1957, no. 41, pl. XXVII
Lent by Mrs. Richard Krautheimer

When Boucher designed a series of five tapestries for the Beauvais looms in 1739, he chose as his subject a folk-tale which had been told many times since antiquity, the story of Psyche. This daughter of a royal family was of such exceptional beauty that she aroused the jealousy of Venus. An oracle commanded that Psyche be taken to the top of a mountain and there abandoned. "Trembling but resigned, Psyche was awaiting on a solitary rock the fulfilment of the oracle, when suddenly she felt herself gently lifted in the arms of Zephyrus, who carried her to a magnificent palace."[1] It was in the palace of love that Psyche displayed her treasures to her jealous sisters. The story goes on to tell of the love of Eros (the Greek *Love*) and Psyche (the Greek *Soul*), and the strange pact which they made: that she was never to look upon her husband's face and that he was always to visit her in the dark of night. Psyche broke the divine taboo and was punished for it, until Zeus took pity on her and made her immortal.

The large painting (10' x 14') which Boucher exhibited in the Salon of 1739, *Zephyr Leading Psyche into the Palace of Love,* was the first of five scenes in the set of the *Story of Psyche* which went on the Beauvais looms in 1741. The painting has not survived, but several drawings for the various tapestries in the set exist, among them this charming group of Zephyr and Psyche which appears at the left of the first tapestry (fig. 20); a study for the figure of Psyche in the *Basketmaker,* the fifth tapestry (Dean Swanson Collection, Minneapolis), and the draped female figure of the nymph in *The Toilet of Psyche.*

The set of tapestries designed by Boucher for the Beauvais looms contained the five scenes he had chosen to illustrate: *Zephyr Leading Psyche into the Palace of Love; The Toilet of Psyche; Psyche Displaying her Treasures to Her Sisters; Psyche Abandoned* and *Psyche at the Basketmaker's.*[2] The episodes were derived from the *"divertissement de cour"* a ballet-opera which Molière, with the help of Corneille, had dramatized in the winter of 1671, and which had been set to music by Lulli. The *Psyche* ballet was danced during the *Carnaval* at the court of Louis XIV and was revived many times in Boucher's day. When Molière's complete works were published in the lavish edition of 1734, Boucher, who did the illustrations, included a charming frontispiece for the *Prologue* to *Psyche*.

Nowhere is Boucher's extraordinary inventiveness of decorative detail, his skilful grouping of figures and his lavish use of rococo architectural ornament so much in evidence as in these exuberant compositions of the late thirties; rarely do his figures display such grace and elegance combined with solid plasticity and clarity of form.

A fine set of the *Psyche* tapestries, comprising all five subjects, is in the Philadelphia Museum of Art; other complete sets are in the Royal Collection, Stockholm and in the Quirinale Palace, Rome.

1. *New Larousse Encyclopedia of Mythology,* London, 1972, p. 132.
2. See Badin, p. 60.

Fig. 20. After Boucher. *Zephyr Leading Psyche into the Palace of Love* (detail). Tapestry. Malibu, The J. Paul Getty Museum

39
The Altar of Friendship
Black chalk heightened with white on blue paper
330 x 260
Lent by Mr. and Mrs. John Canaday

The drawing for which this sheet is a preliminary study appears to be lost, but an engraving by Gilles Demarteau entitled *Autel de l'amitié* (fig. 21, Leymarie no. 75), refers to it as being in the collection of M. de la Haye, the wealthy Fermier Général who was one of Boucher's most important patrons. In the engraving all the details are, of course, carried out with great precision; two cherubs lift a garland toward the altar on which lies a heart, about to be crowned with a wreath of flowers. The allusion to love being sacrificed on the altar of friendship is quite clear, for the cherub at left holds a burning torch to the heart. A bare, withered tree appears symbolically in the background.

In the *première pensée* for the composition, Boucher sketched the cherub's arm at right, then corrected his design and tentatively indicated the figure of the cherub at left. The figure of the draped woman holding the crown is sensitively and beautifully drawn, conveying a sense of harmony between the concept and execution of the theme. It has been suggested that the subject alludes to Madame de Pompadour's altered relationship with Louis XV, which did not diminish the influence the marquise exerted in the king's life, but substituted friendship for physical passion.[1] Since the changed status of Madame de Pompadour as the king's official, but not actual, mistress had become an open secret (eighteenth century memoirs are notoriously unreliable, but a number agree that this took place around 1750), and since Boucher was preoccupied with the iconography of *l'amour* vs. *l'amitié,* it seems safe to surmise that the drawing was indeed intended as an allegory.

A drawing in red chalk entitled *l'Autel de l'Amitié* is listed in Michel (no. 1586) with the comment *a été gravé*; this may have been the drawing from the de la Haye Collection for which the present drawing served as a study. A drawing in the Bourgarel Sale (Paris, June, 15–16, 1922, no. 66, repr.) appears to be a copy after the Demarteau print, as does a drawing in the Witt Library (no. 4206). Another version of the drawing, in the Victoria and Albert Museum, entitled *Scene of Sacrifice with Putti* (Dyce Coll. no. 595) shows two putti reclining before the altar,

Fig. 21. Demarteau, after Boucher.
The Altar of Friendship.
Engraving. Private collection

while the third holds the garland at left. This drawing could quite possibly be an earlier version of the de la Haye drawing, which must have been very fine, judging from the engraved copy and the high quality of all the drawings in the Fermier Général's Collection. Although the *Scene of Sacrifice with Putti* has a certain grave dignity and is competently executed, it lacks the clarity and forcefulness of the preliminary sketch in the Canaday Collection.

1. C. K. Gordon, "Madame de Pompadour, Pigalle and the Iconography of Friendship," *The Art Bulletin,* Sept. 1968, p. 249.

40
The Wedding of the Mandarin
Red chalk
394 x 470
Provenance: L. G. Duke
Exhibited: Northampton, Mass., Smith College Museum,
"Chinoiserie," 1965, no. 3
Lent from the Wolf Collection

To satisfy the French taste for *chinoiserie* in the eighteenth century, Boucher drew and painted numerous subjects *"dans le goût chinois"* which threatened, according to one contemporary critic, to engulf him in that exotic taste entirely.[1] "The eighteenth century," says Hyatt Mayor, "was fascinated by a mostly imaginary Cathay, with a court etiquette more ancient and elaborate than its own, and a practical morality unembittered by the wrangling of priests. Chinoiserie decorations tended to be finicky and improbable, except when Boucher drew Celestials with a generous scale and dreamlike humanity."[2]

The famous *Tenture chinoise* was a set of nine tapestries which Boucher designed for the Beauvais manufactory. He exhibited in the Salon of 1742 the sketches for these tapestries; they were greatly admired for their gay exoticism, and subsequently bought by the Besançon architect Pierre-Antoine Pâris, who bequeathed them to the municipal library of his native city. They are housed today in the Musée des Beaux-Arts at Besançon, one of the few ensembles of Boucher's decorative schemes to have survived intact.

Isolated figures and motifs for the sketches were drawn by Boucher in red or black chalk; *The Wedding of the Mandarin* is one such preparatory study for one of the Besançon sketches (fig. 22). Elaborately detailed, this red chalk drawing is a careful summary of all the elements so freely treated in the painted

Fig. 22. *Chinese Wedding.*
Painting. Besançon, Musée des
Beaux-Arts

sketch. The Besançon designs (translated into cartoons by Du-
mons) were woven a number of times, and can be seen in
excellent examples at The Metropolitan Museum of Art, the
Cincinnati Art Museum and the Minneapolis Institute of Art.
In the eighteenth century, a set was acquired by Madame de
Pompadour, and another set was sent by Louis XV as a gift to
the Emperor K'ang Hsi. One cannot help wondering how the
Celestials responded to seeing themselves in a rococo setting designed by Boucher.

1. Among Boucher's effects were numerous Chinese paintings, bronzes,
porcelains, *pagodes chinoises,* gold and silver ornaments, including a headdress in gold, inlaid with precious stones and pearls. See nos. 631-641,
773-837, in the sale catalog of his effects.
2. A. H. Mayor, *Prints and People,* New York, 1971, no. 589.

41
Episode from the Life of Cyrus the Great
Black chalk and gray wash on buff paper
330 X 390
Lent by The William Hayes Ackland Memorial Art Center,
University of North Carolina, Ackland Fund

The heroes and great figures of antiquity were favorite subjects for paintings and tapestries which called for noble and heroic themes. Historical as well as legendary characters served as models of courage, justice and magnanimity with whom the artists' patrons could identify in a most flattering way. This may account for the popularity of such themes as *The Continence of Scipio, Alexander and the Family of Darius* and episodes from the story of Cyrus the Great.

Previously known as an episode from the story of Alexander, the drawing of a figure seated in majesty, with offerings and captives brought before him, corresponds more closely in subject matter to the theme of *Cyrus and the Daughter of Gobryas,* an obscure story, but beautiful and moving, as told by Xenophon. Gobryas, an Assyrian prince whom Cyrus had conquered, begged the Persian king to come to his castle and receive his homage. "And when they were inside, Gobryas brought out golden goblets, pitchers and vases, all sorts of ornaments, an almost countless pile of darics, and all sorts of treasure in great quantities; and finally he brought out his daughter, a marvel of beauty and stature, but in mourning for her brother who was dead; and he said: 'These treasures, Cyrus, I present to you, and this my daughter I entrust to you to make what disposal of her you may see fit. But we make our prayer to you, I, as I have done already, that you avenge my son, and she that you be the avenger of her brother.' 'Well,' said Cyrus in reply to this, 'I promised you even then that I should do all in my power to avenge you. Now as to these treasures,' said he, 'I accept them, but I give them again to your daughter here and the man who shall marry her'."[1]

A related story is that of *Cyrus and Panthea,* which contains elements that recall the *Continence of Scipio.* The victorious King Cyrus, enthroned in a magnificent palace hall, has brought before him the captured wife of his vanquished enemy Abradates, but he refuses to dishonor the noble captive. The subject of *Cyrus and Panthea* is rarely represented, one of the few known examples being the painting by Pietro da Cortona in the Pitti

Palace. Boucher owned seven drawings by Pietro da Cortona, whose *Cyrus and Panthea* might have been familiar to him from the engraving by the seventeenth century French engraver François Spierre.[2] Although it may have been intended as a project for a painting or tapestry, the drawing of *Cyrus and the Daughter of Gobryas* did not, as far as we know, serve as a preliminary sketch for any other composition.

1. Xenophon, *Cyropaedia,* trans. W. Miller, Cambridge, 1947, bk. IV, ch. 6, p. 397.
2. Cf. Pigler, II, p. 295.

42
Fame and Cupids Holding aloft an Escutcheon
Black chalk
272 x 200
Provenance: Falconet; H. Dreux (sale, Paris, Feb. 3–4, 1870, no. 9)
Bibliography: Michel, no. 981
Exhibited: Boucher, 1957, no. 3, pl. 1; Lafayette, Ind., Purdue University, "Paintings and Drawings, 18th Century French, from the Wildenstein Gallery," 1966, no. 1
Lent by Mrs. Winston F. C. Guest

In this attractive design, two cupids are placing a laurel wreath on an escutcheon which was intended to show the coat-of-arms of the person whose portrait was to be placed within the frame indicated below. The allegorical figures above, a winged cherub blowing a trumpet and holding a circlet (a crown?) in one hand, and a draped female figure resting her right hand on a plumed helmet, would indicate that the design was meant to memorialize a famous soldier, perhaps a marshall of France or a prince of the royal house who had distinguished himself in battle. Frequently, when such a portrait was engraved, (for example, Boucher's portrait of the Maréchal de Lowendal, engraved by Larmessin), the legend would be accompanied by just such allegorical attributes, as well as his coat-of-arms. The female figure, possibly meant to symbolize France, occurs in exactly the same position in a painting by Boucher, engraved by Tilliard.

43
Inspiration
Black and brown chalk and brown wash
210 x 250
Provenance: J. A. Duval le Camus (Lugt 1441)
Exhibited: Iowa City, University of Iowa, "Drawings and
the Human Figure," 1964, no. 66
Lent anonymously

The woman draped in a classical robe and holding a quill pen
might be a muse, composing a tribute to some noble patron of
the arts; all the attributes of painting, sculpture, music and
scholarship are placed in evidence: the palette and paint brushes
on the stool at her left; the terrestrial globe at her right; the
pile of books and the sculptured bust on the table before her,
and the winged seraph, holding a lyre, hovering behind her. The
drawing's theme was part of the basic repertory of eighteenth
century French artists who devised title pages, frontispieces and
dedications for engravings which paid homage to those who
gave encouragement to the arts.

44
Reclining Nude

Red and black chalk heightened with white on blue paper
faded to buff
290 x 378
Provenance: Imperial Library, Winter Palace, Leningrad
(Lugt 2769d); The Hermitage Museum (Lugt 2681a; sale,
Leipzig, Apr. 29, 1931, no. 30); Robert Treat Paine II
Bibliography: A. A. Mitchell, "A Drawing by François
Boucher," *Bulletin of the Museum of Fine Arts,* Boston, 42,
Feb. 1944, pp. 11–12, repr.; Slatkin, 1972, p. 267, fig. 5
Exhibited: Cambridge, Fogg Art Museum, "French Drawings
and Prints of the Eighteenth Century," 1934, no. 4; Boston,
Museum of Fine Arts, "Art in New England," 1939, no. 143,
pl. LXIX; Paris, Orangerie, no. 33, pl. 43
Lent by the Museum of Fine Arts, Boston, Gift of Robert
Treat Paine II

The personal library of the Tsars of Russia contained, besides
books and manuscripts, a collection of prints and drawings
which bore the Imperial stamp — a crown (Lugt 2769d). The
drawings were eventually incorporated into the collection of The
Hermitage Museum which owned a number of outstanding
paintings and drawings by Boucher, most of them acquired by
Catherine the Great from her friend and counselor, General
Betzkoy. This wealthy connoisseur spent many years in Paris as
unofficial ambassador of the empress whose taste for French art
he managed to satisfy by shipping back to Russia boatloads of
fine French furniture and works of art. Himself a collector and
president of the Académie des Beaux-Arts of St. Petersburg
(which offered Boucher an honorary membership), General
Betzkoy disposed of his collection of drawings to the empress
in 1767 (cf. Lugt 2878a). Eventually they became part of The
Hermitage in Leningrad, but after 1928 the Soviet government
sold an important group of French drawings at auction in
Germany.

The *Reclining Nude* bears both the stamp of the Winter
Palace Library and The Hermitage Museum. It is one of the
showpieces by means of which Boucher established a market for
drawing among the collectors in France and abroad. The drawings was engraved in sanguine *en manière de crayon* by Louis
Marin Bonnet.

45
Diana and Callisto

Black chalk
233 x 340
Collector's mark (Marc Bernheim), lower left
Provenance: Randon de Boisset (sale, Paris, Feb. 27, 1777, no.
338); Sireuil (sale, Paris, Dec. 3, 1781, no. 84); Marc Bernheim
Lent by Mr. and Mrs. Robert Scheiner

In Ovid's day, the legends of classical Greece had lost their
sacred character and become charming romances in which the
gods behaved as irresponsibly and irrationally as humans. The
tale of Callisto, the Arcadian nymph whom Jupiter desired and
betrayed, evokes pity for the unfortunate victim and resentment
against the god who would not control his unbridled passion.
Although innocently wronged, Callisto must brave the wrath
of her mistress Diana whose favorite companion she has been,
and who now rejects her, for she who has been violated by
Jupiter and bears his child can no longer bathe in the sacred
spring. The story is brought to a dramatic climax when Juno,
raging against the infidelity of Jupiter, turns Callisto into a bear,
whom Jupiter eventually transports into the heavens, to shine
forever as a bright constellation in the firmament.

Boucher made several sketches of the episode which Ovid
relates in Book II of the *Metamorphoses*:

> Now the moon's horns were filling out to complete
> their ninth circle, when the goddess wearied with hunt-
> ing in the fierce heat of the sun, came to a cool grove,
> from which there flowed a murmuring stream that rip-
> pled over its smooth sandy bed. Diana exclaimed with
> pleasure at the sight, and dipped her foot in the water:
> delighted with this too, she called to her companions:
> 'There is no one here to see us—let us undress, and
> bathe in the brook.' The Arcadian maiden blushed. All
> the rest took off their garments, while she alone sought
> excuses to delay. As she hesitated, the others pulled off
> her tunic, and at one and the same time revealed her
> body and her crime. She stood dismayed, and with her
> hands vainly tried to cover up the evidence of her
> guilt. But Diana cried: 'Off with you! Do not defile
> this sacred spring!' and ordered her to withdraw from
> her company.[1]

In this handsome drawing Boucher projected a very elaborate
composition which was never executed. Two other drawings

dealing with the same subject, one of which had belonged to his son-in-law, the painter Baudoin (sale, Feb. 15, 1770), the other to the H. Michel-Lévy Collection (sale May 12, 1919) were also sketches that were never realized as painted compositions. The actual episode of Jupiter in the guise of Diana embracing the nymph Callisto was painted by Boucher several times, notably in the picture shown in the Salon of 1765 (now in the Linsky Collection).

The history of the present drawing is of particular interest. It was owned by the *Receveur général des finances*, Randon de Boisset, whom Boucher accompanied on a trip to the Low Countries in 1766. At the de Boisset Sale in 1777 it was acquired by M. de Sireuil, former gentleman of the king's bedchamber, a patron and great admirer of Boucher who owned no less than 187 drawings by the artist, and spent long hours with him in his studio, watching him paint.

1. Ovid, *Metamorphoses,* trans. M. M. Innes, London, 1971, bk. II, p. 62.

Fig. 23. *Diana Resting after the Hunt.* Painting. Paris, Musée du Louvre

46
A Seated Nude

Red chalk, heightened with white, on pink paper
318 x 267
Bibliography: C. Virch, *Master Drawings in the Collection of Walter C. Baker,* New York, 1962, no. 74
Exhibited: Slatkin, 1959, no. 44, repr.; New York, The Metropolitan Museum of Art, "The Walter C. Baker Collection of Drawings," 1960
Lent by the Estate of Walter C. Baker

The year 1742 saw Boucher fully launched on a successful career. In April he received a royal stipend; shortly thereafter, his work for the opera began. He also produced a series of colorful imaginative *chinoiserie* designs for the Beauvais tapestry works which he exhibited at the Salon of 1742. Several of his beautiful landscapes painted in the vicinity of Beauvais were also included in the exhibition, as were two paintings of sparkling beauty and freshness: *Leda and the Swan,* now in the Nationalmuseum, Stockholm, and *Diana Resting after the Hunt,* now in the Louvre (fig. 23).

The *Diana,* which bears the date 1742, is based on this life study in the Baker Collection, a delicate and appealing work from Boucher's most creative period.

47
Diana

Red, black and white chalk on buff paper
387 x 323
Provenance: Sir Thomas Lawrence (Lugt 2445); Niewenhuys;
Heseltine (Lugt 1507); Mary Benjamin Rogers
Bibliography: Michel, no. 491, as *Diane sortant du bain;*
Heseltine, 1900, no. 18; Heseltine, 1913, no. 6, repr.;
Ananoff, no. 771
Exhibited: London, "National Loan Exhibition," 1909–1910,
no. 73
Lent anonymously

Fig. 24. *Diana after the Hunt.*
Painting. Paris, Musée Cognacq-Jay

Diana after the Hunt, painted as an overdoor decoration for
the Salle de l'Horloge at Versailles, shows the seated figure of
the goddess, untying the sandal on her right foot, her left foot
already plunging into the cooling water of a forest pool. Her
three companion nymphs are seated at the right, while all about
are the quivers of arrows and the spoils of the hunt. This study
for the figure of Diana is mistakenly called by Michel (no. 491)
Etude pour le tableau du Musée du Louvre, but the painting is
actually in the Musée Cognacq-Jay, Paris (fig. 24). The date
1745, which appears with Boucher's signature in the left foreground of the painting, may be assigned to the drawing as well.
A study in black chalk for the entire composition (Michel, no.
745) was in the Beurdeley Sale of 1905. Here again, Michel con-
fuses the painting *Diana Resting after the Hunt* which was done
three years earlier, and is now in the Louvre (fig. 23), with the
Cognacq-Jay picture. A study for the Louvre *Diana* is in the
Baker Collection (pl. 46).

48
Reclining Nude

Red, black and white chalk on blue-green paper
227 x 320
Provenance: Duke of Leeds; C. Fairfax Murray; Walter
Burns (sale, London, Sotheby's, Mar. 22, 1923, no. 7, repr.);
Mrs. C. I. Stralem
Bibliography: Art Digest, July 1, 1940, repr. p. 40
Exhibited: Buffalo, Albright-Knox Art Gallery, "Master
Exhibited: Buffalo, Albright Art Gallery, "Master Drawings,"
Drawings," 1935, no. 70, repr.; San Francisco, 1940, p. 92, no.
406; London, Royal Academy, 1968, no. 99, fig. 120
Lent by Mr. and Mrs. Donald S. Stralem

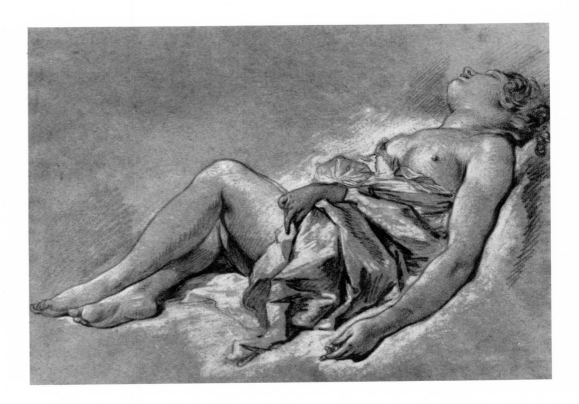

Fig. 25. *Diana and Callisto.*
Painting. San Francisco, The Fine
Arts Museums of San Francisco, The
Roscoe and Margaret Oakes Collection

Two of the most attractive ensembles which Boucher painted
for Madame de Pompadour are now in American museums—the
small boudoir with its enchanting panels of children at various
occupations in The Frick Collection, and the suite of five pastoral scenes from the Château de Bellevue, now in the California
Palace of the Legion of Honor, San Francisco. A quintet of
ravishing beauties, celebrated in classical mythology, is portrayed
in the latter suite. In one of these paintings, Diana the huntress
is resting in a forest clearing, attended by her favorite nymph,
Callisto, who teases the sleeping goddess (fig. 25). The *Reclining Nude* is a study for the figure of Diana or possibly a study
after it, for the highly finished drawing of a beautiful half-clad
woman in a languorous pose was exactly the sort of work for
which Boucher's fashionable clients clamored, and which his
engravers, as he put it, snatched out of his hands. The drawing
was engraved by Gilles Demarteau who added a few touches
of his own: a rose at the goddess' feet, a bracelet on her wrist,
a plump, tasseled pillow at her back (Leymarie, no. 197). The
painting *Diana and Callisto* is dated 1745, which is the date
ascribed to the drawing in the Stralem Collection.

49
Diana Attended by Her Nymphs in a Glade

Black, red and white chalk on buff paper
204 x 305
Provenance: Groult; Anonymous sale, London, Christie's,
Apr. 7, 1970, no. 71, repr.
Lent anonymously

The theme of the goddess Diana was a favorite subject with Boucher who delighted in depicting the beauty of the female nude in a poetic woodland setting. His most famous version of the subject is the *Diana Resting after the Hunt* in the Louvre (fig. 23). The pose of Diana and her companion nymph in the Louvre picture clearly derives from the figures in this drawing, which also represents the goddess after the drama of the chase. In the final, painted version, Boucher has reduced the number of nymphs to one and placed more emphasis upon the accessory details of still life, hunting dogs and drapery. He has preserved the original wooded landscape background, but he has enriched the composition by adding a stream near where the goddess is seated. A life study for the seated figure of Diana is in the Walter Baker Collection in New York (pl. 46).

The study *Diana Attended by Her Nymphs in a Glade* demonstrates Boucher's ability to work out his *première pensée* in a sketchy, tentative manner, which subsequently takes shape in a fully realized though often somewhat altered composition.

50
Mercury

Red and white chalk on tan antique laid paper
336 × 355
Bibliography: Slatkin, 1967, p. 56, pl. 48; *Wallace Collection Catalogues, Pictures and Drawings,* London, 1968, p. 40, no. P487
Exhibited: Daniels Collection, 1968, no. 20, repr.
Lent by David Daniels

Fig. 26. *Mercury Confiding the Infant Bacchus to the Nymphs.*
Oil sketch. Lent anonymously

Study for the painting *Mercury Confiding the Infant Bacchus to the Nymphs* in the Wallace Collection. The painting, together with its pendant *The Rape of Europa,* also in the Wallace Collection, was engraved by Aveline. Early in the nineteenth century, these pictures were attributed to François Lemoyne, Boucher's teacher, but unlike some of Boucher's early works which do indeed display many elements found in Lemoyne—his boldness and luminosity of color, the baroque sweep of his design—the *Mercury* as well as the *Europa* already have all the characteristics of Boucher's mature period.

Mercury was the most versatile of the Graeco-Roman pantheon. A divine jack-of-all-trades, he escorted souls to Hades, served as the tricky patron of thieves, and above all performed, on his winged feet ("foot-feather'd Mercury," Keats called him) numerous errands for Jupiter and the other Olympians. The most famous delivery made by this messenger of the gods was to Circe's island, where he provided Ulysses with a magic flower to safeguard him from the witch's sorcery.

In the Wallace Collection painting for which this drawing of Mercury is a study, he is again following Jupiter's orders. He confides the infant Bacchus (the fruit of one of Jupiter's numerous indiscretions, and thus the object of Juno's rage) to the nymphs of Mount Nysa, to be raised in secret. From this incident derives the constellation of the Hyades, into which Jupiter's gratitude transformed the faithful nurses, and the invention of wine which (thanks to Mercury) Bacchus lived to discover on the mountain.

The theme of *Mercury Confiding the Infant Bacchus to the Nymphs,* based on an episode from Ovid (*Metamorphoses* III, 14–15), was a favorite subject with French artists throughout the seventeenth and eighteenth centuries.[1] The drawing of Mercury is typical of the kind of study sheet which Boucher sketched in preparation for his most ambitious compositions of the forties

and fifties, and it is to that period that it should be assigned. Studies for several other figures in the composition exist, as well as a preliminary oil sketch for the painting (fig. 26).

1. Pigler, II, pp. 42-43.

51

Venus and Mercury

Black chalk and gray wash on buff paper
205 x 290
Signed, lower left: *Boucher*
Provenance: Victor Koch
Lent anonymously

This airy sketch of the goddess of Love surrounded by *amoretti* and attended by Mercury, messenger of the gods, may have been intended as a design for an overdoor decoration, as indicated by the faint suggestion of an arched top which appears in the drawing. The incident depicted is perhaps that in which Mercury was bidden by Jupiter to conduct the three goddesses, Venus, Juno and Minerva to the shepherd Paris so that he could award the golden apple to the fairest of the three.

The sketchy use of black chalk and gray wash is a combination which Boucher frequently makes use of to convey the idea of aerial perspective in a ceiling or overdoor design.

52
Bacchanale
Oil on paper
305 x 191
Exhibited: Tokyo, Fukuoka, Kyoto, "Exposition d'Art
Français au Japon," 1954–1955, no. 54
Lent by Mr. and Mrs. Henry F. Harrison

This bacchanalian scene whose participants are surprisingly sober in mien, if not in action, is dashed off with Boucher's customary élan. The oil sketches, generally done on paper, were almost always an intermediary step between a drawing and a painted composition; they show the artist thinking out a project with his brush. It is the painter's rapid-fire conversation when describing a lively scene. Features are indicated with a flick of the brush, a dash of Chinese white here and there is used to highlight the rich, dark tones of the oil, thinly applied. Although similar groups can be found in the background of some Beauvais tapestry cartoons, this particular group of nymphs with clashing cymbals does not occur in any other composition by Boucher.

53
Venus and Cupid

Colored chalks and pastel on buff paper
363 x 254
Signed and dated, lower left: *J. Boucher 1759*. Glomy stamp,
bottom center (Lugt 1085)
Provenance: Marquis de Biron; Marius Paulme (Lugt 1910;
sale, Paris, May 13, 1929, no. 26, pl. 21)
Bibliography: Goncourt, p. 189
Exhibited: Providence, Rhode Island School of Design, 1931;
Omaha, Joslyn Art Museum, 1941–1946
Lent anonymously

One of Boucher's most seductive nudes, this Venus on the clouds
is, according to the Paulme catalog, being divested of her last
veil: "Elle abaisse son regard vers L'Amour qui, la tête renversée,
s'efforce, de ses deux bras élevés, à arracher le dernier voile qui
la recouvrait encore." However, the title under which the drawing was engraved by J. B. Michel, *L'Amour Modeste,* suggests
that the little cupid was attempting to cover rather than uncover
the nude body of the goddess. Was this another attempt at
modesty on the part of the engraver?[1]

1. J. B. Michel (1748–1804) engraved a number of Boucher's works.

54
The Birth of Venus

Black chalk heightened with white chalk on gray paper
323 x 445
Inscribed, lower left: *f. Boucher*
Provenance: Edwin Bryant Crocker
Bibliography: F. W. Kent, *Crocker Art Gallery Catalogue of Collections,* Sacramento, 1964, repr. p. 95; P. Rosenberg, "Twenty French Drawings in Sacramento," *Master Drawings,* 8, no. 1, 1970, p. 39; *Master Drawings from Sacramento,* Sacramento, 1971, listed p. 148
Exhibited: Davis, University of California at Davis, "Classical Narratives in Master Drawings," 1972, no. 20, repr.
Lent by the E. B. Crocker Art Gallery

In the Salon of 1740 Boucher exhibited a very large painting, *La Naissance de Vénus,* which is now in the Nationalmuseum, Stockholm. The drawing in the Crocker Art Gallery has been referred to as a study for this picture, but it is, in fact, a preliminary sketch for an altogether different composition with the same title, formerly in the collection of the Comtesse de Béarn (fig. 27). Preparatory studies exist for almost all the figures in this composition: a drawing for the central figure of Venus is in the collection of Baron Robert von Hirsch (fig. 28), while the reclining nymph on the extreme right is the drawing in The British Museum (fig. 29). The spirited drawing in the Crocker Art Gallery, which illustrates once again Boucher's method in carefully preparing his elaborate compositions, is beyond question the preliminary design for this handsome painting. The group of gesticulating nymphs at the extreme right in the drawing has been omitted in the painting, which substitutes a triton blowing on a conch shell, providing a nice balance for the triton at the extreme left.

Fig. 27. *The Birth of Venus.*
Painting. Formerly Béarn Collection

Fig. 28. *Study for Venus.*
Drawing. Baron Robert von Hirsch
Collection

Fig. 29. *Study for Reclining Nymph.*
Drawing. London, The British
Museum

55
Eros and Psyche

Pen and brown wash over black and red chalk
Oval, 240 x 315
Provenance: Jean Dubois (sale, Paris, Mar. 21–22, 1927, no. 4,
repr.); Marius Paulme (sale, Paris, Mar. 13, 1929, no. 19,
repr.); Anonymous sale, Geneva, Rauch, June 13–15, 1960,
no. 44
Bibliography: Carlson, 1966, pp. 161, 162, pl. 23
Exhibited: New York, Wildenstein, 1963, no. 49
Lent by The Art Institute of Chicago, The Joseph and
Helen Regenstein Collection

Although this drawing has generally been referred to as *Venus and Amor,*[1] it scarcely seems possible that the goddess of love who is always shown in an attitude of protectiveness or authority over her little son would be awaiting his amorous gesture. It seems more reasonable to assume that the flying figures about to embrace are Eros and Psyche (the Greek *Love* and the Greek *Soul*) whose story, appearing first in *The Golden Ass* by Apuleius, the only complete surviving Latin novel, has been a favorite since late antiquity. Boccaccio made the tale popular, interpreting it allegorically; Raphael illustrated it in his famous Farnesina frescoes.

We have referred to the story of Cupid (or Eros) and Psyche earlier (no. 38) and we return to it once more, recognizing in the flying figures surrounded by cloud-borne putti, the characters of this ancient tale. The final bliss of the couple's hard-won union, which some writers saw as symbolic of the soul's attainment to Love or Beauty, is thus envisioned by Keats in his "Ode to Psyche":

> Surely I dreamt today, or did I see
>   The winged Psyche with awaken'd eyes?
> I wander'd in a forest thoughtlessly,
>   And, on the sudden, fainting with surprise,
> Saw two fair creatures, couched side by side.

Boucher worked the figures into a swirling arabesque, lending a dynamic quality to this illusionistic design for a ceiling. Stylistically the drawing of *Eros and Psyche* is related to another ceiling design by Boucher which Jean-Charles François engraved in one of his first attempts at aquatint, in 1758.[2] The pen and wash medium of Boucher's design logically suggested the aquatint process, and it is not surprising therefore to find the Abbé de St. Non also using aquatint when he engraved the *Eros and*

Psyche design in 1766. Like scores of other designs for architectural decorations which Boucher seems to have tossed off with lightning speed, these ceilings remained, as far as we know, unrealized projects.

1. Cf. Carlson, p. 161.
2. Repr. by J. Herold, *Jean-Charles François, Catalogue de l'oeuvre gravé,* Paris, 1931, pl. 20.

56

A Farmyard

Black chalk heightened with white on blue paper
346 x 480
Signed, lower left: *f. Boucher*
Provenance: Sireuil(?); A. Koster (sale, Leipzig, Nov. 13, 1924, no. 89, pl. 8); Cafmeyer; Lucien Guiraud; Anonymous sale, Paris, Mar. 15, 1968, no. 7, pl. 1
Exhibited: Paris, Cailleux, 1951, *"Le Dessin Français de Watteau à Prud'hon,"* 1951, no. 24
Lent by Yale University Art Gallery, Everett V. Meeks B. A. 1901 and Paul Mellon B. A. 1929 Fund

The back door of a farmhouse through which two children peer as though startled by an intruder. A wobbly ladder leading to the hayloft leans against the adjoining barn. A clutter of wooden tubs, straw baskets, an iron kettle, an earthenware pot, fill the foreground. Vines trail along the cottage walls; the cage of a dove or songbird hangs suspended on the wall in a patch of sunlight. All the elements of this rustic corner recall Boucher's interest in the peasant scenes of the seventeenth century Dutch painters; one has only to compare this drawing of a French farmyard with a drawing of a barn by Adriaen van Ostade or Herman Saftleven to realize the extent to which Boucher was indebted to the art of the Low Countries, yet he managed to give this scene a lyric quality, as though it were intended as a backdrop against which some rustic idyll might be played.

The Yale drawing of a farmyard may quite possibly be the item referred to in the Sireuil catalog (Dec. 3, 1781, no. 101) as "Un autre Paysage au crayon noir et blanc, sur papier bleu, representant l'interieur d'une Ferme. Il est riche de composition, et d'une touche spirituelle. Hauteur 12 pouces, largeur 18 pouces." Stylistically related to the Yale *Farmyard* is Boucher's drawing of the interior of a barn in the Nationalmuseum, Stockholm, which also has strong affinities with the landscape art of seventeenth century Holland.

57
Wooded Landscape with Boy Fishing

Black and white chalk on blue paper
300 x 443
Provenance: Jean Gigoux; Marquis de Fourquevaux;
Delestre (sale, Paris, Apr. 18–20, 1876, no. 276)
Bibliography: Goncourt, p. 208; Michel, no. 1960; Vallery-
Radot, pl. 44; Carlson, 1966, pp. 157–163, repr.; Y. Bruand
and M. Hébert, *Inventaire du fonds français, graveurs du
XVIIIe siècle,* Paris, 1970, XIV, no. 22; Jean-Richard, cf. no.
48; C. Baer, *Landscape Drawings,* New York, 1973, pp. 25,
26, 244, repr. p. 245
Exhibited: New York, Wildenstein, 1963, no. 48, pl. XVIII
Lent by The Art Institute of Chicago, The Joseph and
Helen Regenstein Collection

About ten miles south of Paris on the road to Orléans, an aqueduct built in Roman times (Arcus Juliani) gave its name to the village of Arcueil. Here, during the first half of the eighteenth century, stood the château of the Prince de Guise, with its magnificent gardens renowned throughout Europe. The aqueduct, rebuilt in the seventeenth century, served as a monumental backdrop for the princely estate and became the recurrent motif in the sketches which Oudry and Portail, Boucher, Natoire and Wille made in the gardens. Stately terraces, handsome avenues of trees leading to broad vistas, pools and playing fountains, leafy arbors and shady pergolas covered with trellises, brooks and rustic bridges, were the components of these gardens, landscaped in radiant beauty. Nothing remains of them now, for the château was dismantled in 1752, and the park abandoned; the aqueduct, rebuilt in the nineteenth century, is all but lost in the smoke of an industrial suburb. But the sketches made by Boucher and his contemporaries before the gardens were abandoned recall the lost beauty of this sylvan retreat.

Boucher made many drawings in the park at Arcueil, some of them accurate renderings of a site he sketched, others based on some motif he chose in the garden and worked up into an imaginary landscape, a *paysage composé.* He delighted in the formal arrangements of smooth, hedge-enclosed lawns, the well-kept *parterres,* clipped trees, statuary on classic balustrades and huge, flower-filled urns; but he also sketched the more casual aspects of gardens, the natural beauty of which appealed to him. After the gardens were allowed to fall into ruin, Boucher, along with other artists, continued to visit Arcueil; "Partout on ne rencontroit que dessinateurs", wrote a contemporary. Some of these drawings capture the melancholy air of a woodland scene with dense shrubbery, gnarled trees with fallen limbs and weeds straggling across a rocky path.

Shortly after the park at Arcueil was deserted, the engraver Chedel advertised[1] two etchings he had made after Boucher drawings with Arcueil themes: the *Aqueduct at Arcueil* (now in the Albertina) which he entitled *Le Pont Rustique* and the *Wooded Landscape with Boy Fishing* (now in The Art Institute of Chicago) which he called *Le Pêcheur.* Chedel had etched a number of Boucher's landscape drawings, including his *quatre Paysages dessinés d'après nature,* but his highly finished prints cannot convey the airy, poetic quality of Boucher's sensitive sketches, such as the *Wooded Landscape* in Chicago. That this was not an imaginary, but an actual site would seem to be borne out by the fact that Boucher sketched it also from a different angle in a drawing which shows the boy standing on the bridge instead, as in the Chicago drawing, fishing from it. Still another drawing, also in the Albertina (Inv. 12191) shows the same spot from still another angle, with the trellis structure behind the bridge, and a woman in the foreground, washing clothes in the little brook.

1. The advertisements appeared in the *Annonces* of April 25, 1753, and in the *Mercure* of April 1753.
Illustration overleaf

73

58
Landscape with Rustic Cottage
Black chalk
315 x 470
Lent by the Art Institute of Chicago, The Joseph and
Helen Regenstein Collection

Landscape was the background of most compositions which Boucher painted. He almost invariably chose to sketch some picturesque site which could serve as a setting for his pastorales, using the humble elements of the countryside to build up a composite backdrop of idyllic rural life, against which his nymphs and shepherds, gods and peasants, played their eternal charades.

If the landscapes in Boucher's painted compositions were theatrical backdrops in which local color gave way to mysterious blues and unreal greens, with trees spiraling upward like Gothic cathedrals, and flowers, ferns and shrubbery piled up in rich profusion, the drawings of actual sites which appealed to him and which he sketched *d'après nature,* were authentic records of the French countryside—a quiet river bank, a peasant cottage, a farmyard, a grist mill, a dovecote.

A rustic scene like the farmyard in which a barn with thatched roof occupies the center must have been a familiar sight, often encountered on his trips through the French countryside, but the nostalgic charm which pervades the *Landscape with Rustic Cottage* surely derives from the seventeenth century Dutch landscapes which Boucher admired and collected.

59
Thatched Mill Cottage with Two Trees at the Edge of a Stream

Black chalk and pale gray wash on gray paper
220 X 312
Provenance: Probably Blondel Dazaincourt
Bibliography: Tenth Report to the Fellows of The Pierpont Morgan Library 1960, New York, 1960, p. 62, repr.
Lent by The Pierpont Morgan Library, Gift of the Fellows

Boucher's work has been characterized so frequently as artificial that his love of nature, revealed in his landscape drawings, comes almost as a complete surprise. Yet from his earliest student days in Italy, when he took long walks in the Roman *campagna* with his fellow students, he never missed an opportunity to sketch outdoors. Later on, when he traveled to Beauvais with Oudry (in the thirties) or journeyed by coach to Orléans and Blois, and on his many trips to the various country estates of Madame de Pompadour, or when he visited the gardens at Arcueil, he never failed to observe nature with a keen and fresh eye, delighting in the charms of the French countryside and recording its intimate aspects with an almost romantic fervor.

Boucher's drawing *Thatched Mill Cottage with Two Trees at the Edge of a Stream*, a notable example of this particular genre, was engraved by Jean Hoüel under rather interesting circumstances. Engraving as a hobby occupied much the same place in the eighteenth century that photography does today. Scores of wealthy amateurs took lessons in printmaking from professional engravers, and since the amateurs usually owned or had access to fine collections of paintings and drawings, this turned out well for everyone concerned; it gave the artists access to the great collections, and the owners profited from the lessons they received at the hands of skilled professionals. Blondel Dazincourt, son of the financier and art collector Blondel de Gagny, and himself an avid collector and great admirer of Boucher's work, arranged to take lessons in engraving from Jean Hoüel, one of the gifted young assistants in the renowned workshop of the engraver Le Bas. Since Blondel Dazaincourt owned, among other works of art, 500 drawings by Boucher, Hoüel did not lack subjects to engrave; among his prints are two of Boucher's most attractive landscape drawings, the *Thatched Mill Cottage with Two Trees* in The Pierpont Morgan Library and its companion, the *Farmhouse* in the Albertina. The print of the Albertina drawing is dedicated by Hoüel to his pupil Blondel Dazaincourt, while its pendant, the print after the Morgan Library drawing, is dedicated to Dazaincourt's sister-in-law, Madame de la Haye Dazaincourt, a distinguished collector in her own right. Both prints are dated 1759; the likelihood is that both drawings after which the prints were done belonged to the Dazaincourt family.

1. Y. Bruand and M. Hébert, *Inventaire du Fonds Français, Graveurs du XVIIIe siècle*, XI, Paris, 1970, p. 388.

60

Study of a Goat
Black chalk heightened with white on blue paper
243 x 293
Exhibited: New York, Knoedler, "The Artist and the
Animal," 1968, no. 52, repr. p. 46
Lent by Laura Slatkin

The pastoral idyll was the eighteenth century's idealized version of real life. "When Boucher descended from Olympus", wrote the Goncourts, "his imagination found refreshment in pastoral subjects. These he painted in the only manner that was then permitted: he banished from his idylls *'that particular crudity that is always somewhat distasteful'.*"[1] A rural world in which barefoot shepherdesses, prettily dressed, sat in a forest enclosure, holding flower-filled baskets, dreamily reading their love letters, while sheep rested at their feet and goats calmly surveyed the scene—this was the world of make-believe in which Boucher's patrons masqueraded as *"le berger galant"* and *"la bergère et son troupeau"* in a setting filled with *"les charmes de la vie champêtre"*. If the starving peasants and ragged goatherds were not his real models, at least the cows and sheep, the goats and farmyard fowl could be drawn from life, and so make the landscape of fantasy assume an air of reality.

Boucher's animal studies are free, direct and utterly convincing. His early landscapes, much influenced by Dutch genre, are full of farmyard animals such as those in the drawings in the Nationalmuseum, Stockholm—the shaggy goats, the cow, the donkey, the rooster.[2] To his mythologies belong the drawing of a bull (Berlin Printroom), a study for the *Rape of Europa* in the Louvre, and the drawings of horses (Albertina) which are spirited studies for the Fontainebleau ceiling, *The Chariot of Apollo*. The *Study of a Goat* is familiar from many of his pastoral compositions, but the browsing animal is most easily recognizable in a scene of two shepherdesses beside a sculptured fountain, *La Confidence*,[3] and in The Frick Collection's *Spring*.

1. Goncourt, p. 147 [trans.].
2. A. Gauffin and R. Hoppe, *François Boucher, Malmö*, 1928-30, repr. pls. XXXIII and ff.
3. Marius Paulme Sale, Paris, May 13, 1929, no. 21, pl. 16.

61
Saddled Donkey

Black, red and white chalks on blue-gray tinted paper
303 x 467
Bibliography: Sixteenth Report to the Fellows of The Pierpont Morgan Library, 1969–1971, New York, 1973, pp. 105, 106, 110, note by F. Stampfle
Lent by The Pierpont Morgan Library, purchased as the Gift of Mr. and Mrs. Carl Stern

Boucher's market and farm scenes were not complete without their donkeys, modest animals, waiting patiently for the load they were to carry. Perhaps their docile nature made it easy to sketch them, or perhaps they were more numerous in the French countryside in Boucher's day than they are in our own; at any rate, he introduced them into his *Aller au Marché, Retour du Marché* and *Scène de Campagne* paintings as picturesque *staffage.* More elegant donkeys, richly caparisoned with plumes, ribbons, blinkers and even floral decorations appear in the pastorales, led by shepherdesses, dainty ladies or frolicking children. Of the *Saddled Donkey,* Felice Stampfle writes: "With this drawing one cannot but assume that the draughtsman worked in the presence of his model. It is "Boucher flamand"—in contrast to "Boucher français" and "Boucher italien"—to use Edmond de Goncourt's words, who rendered the patient little jenny with such fidelity and feeling, observing the rounded rump and flank, the musculature of the forequarters, the straggly hair of tail, ears and nostrils, along with the details of bridle and saddle. In particular, he noted the sturdily planted slender legs and the tiny feet with the elongated hooves of the unshod animal."

62
Bacchus and Ariadne: Design for a Fan Leaf

Red and black chalk heightened with white on buff paper
Semicircular; 225 x 435
Inscribed, bottom center: *francois Bouche*
Bibliography: Popham and Fenwick, p. 158, no. 223, repr.
Lent by The National Gallery of Canada

At the beginning of the nineteenth century, when Boucher's work had fallen into disfavor, he was sometimes condescendingly referred to as a decorator of fans and snuff boxes. Modern taste, though oriented in an altogether different direction, cannot help but admire the creative imagination and skill of these designs which could easily be enlarged to fill the space above the door of a palace. The same verve, the same minute attention to craftsmanship informs both the *bibelots* and the tapestry cartoons. The composition of *Bacchus and Ariadne* was used in a tapestry cartoon which was woven at Beauvais in 1749 as part of the series *Les Amours des Dieux (Loves of the Gods)*. All the elements which are present in the tapestry, while much more detailed and elaborate, are also indicated in the charming fan leaf design: the central figures of Bacchus and Ariadne surrounded by nymphs and putti against a background of classical architecture.

The subject was exceptionally popular with French artists, including Vouet, Poussin, Le Brun, as well as most of Boucher's contemporaries.[1] Bacchus (the Greek god Dionysus) discovered Ariadne, the daughter of King Minos, asleep on the island of Naxos, where Theseus had brought her from Crete. There he had abandoned her and left her to her grief. The arrival of Bacchus consoled her and shortly afterwards they were married at a joyous ceremony attended by all the Olympians.

The painting, now lost, which served as a model for the Bacchus and Ariadne tapestry must have been very beautiful, as far as we can judge, for it contained a wealth of decorative elements which Boucher used to build up his elaborate compositions. Studies are extant for several figures, among them the child at the extreme right, holding a gold or silver platter (Albertina) and the nymph and sleeping putto at left (Louvre, Cabinet des Dessins).

1. See Badin, p. 61.

63
Three Nymphs

Black and white chalk on brown paper
264 x 360
Signed and dated, lower right: *f. Boucher 1749*
Collector's mark Glomy at lower right (Lugt 1119)
Provenance: T. Edward Hanley
Bibliography: Vallery-Radot, pl. 59
Exhibited: New York, Wildenstein, "Paintings and Drawings
from the Hanley Collection," 1961, no. 39, repr. p. 29; New
York, Gallery of Modern Art, Philadelphia Museum of Art,
and The Denver Art Museum, "Selections from The
Collection of Dr. and Mrs. T. Edward Hanley," 1967–1968
Lent by the Achenbach Foundation for Graphic Arts,
California Palace of the Legion of Honor

When Boucher boasted that he no longer needed a model for
his nudes since he could draw them from memory, he was
probably referring to the countless nymphs his crayon invented
and drew without apparent effort. The central figures in his
mythological compositions invariably had an entourage of
nymphs, naiads, tritons, river gods, satyrs and cupids, disposed,
singly or in clusters, as the need arose, like ornaments on a
lady's gown. The group of three nymphs with an urn from which
water flows is one of many such variations on the theme of the
female form. The date 1749 inscribed on the drawing is sig-
nificant: it is the year Boucher designed his most famous set of
tapestries for Beauvais: *Les Amours des Dieux.* The eighth
subject in this series, *Venus and Vulcan,*[1] contains the group of
three nymphs floating in the clouds, companions to Venus in
her chariot. The composition must have pleased Boucher, for
he singled it out and repeated it several times, with some variations.

1. Badin, p. 61.

64

Boreas and Oreithyia
Black chalk
346 x 302
Provenance: Anonymous sale, Paris, May 15, 1897, no. 10;
Trézel (sale, Paris, May 17, 1935, no. 18); Corinna Kavanagh (sale,
London, Sotheby's, Mar. 11, 1964, no. 227, repr.)
Bibliography: Michel, no. 557, as *Enlèvement d'une nymphe;*
Ananoff, 872
Lent by David Rust

Among the tapestries which Boucher designed for the Beauvais manufactory was a series known as *Les Amours des Dieux (The Loves of the Gods).*[1] This series was based on nine episodes from the *Metamorphoses* of Ovid and included the loves of Ariadne and Bacchus, Neptune and Amymone, Mars and Venus, and the story of Boreas and Oreithyia.

Boreas, the son of the Titan Astraeus and of Aurora, was the powerful North Wind. He loved the nymph Oreithyia and tried to woo her in gentle fashion, but he was violent by nature and unable to win her love.

> Yet when he found his gentleness meant nothing
> He whipped up anger in his usual style
> And said, 'I've earned defeat, for my true manner
> Is one of wildness and cold rage.'[2]

With these words he seized the nymph and abducted her.

The ferocious nature of the North Wind with his huge wings and violently distorted features bearing aloft the helpless nymph is the strong central focus in the tapestry. In the drawing, the nymph Oreithyia, her arms outflung in despair, is borne by Boreas in powerful embrace while cherubs cling to her, and her startled companions, gesturing wildly, remain earthbound below.

> Boreas raised his wings and with their beating
> Clapped a great blast on earth and tipped wide ocean;
> He trailed his cloak across high-peaked mountains,
> And swept the ground. Then his shroud of darkness
> His dusky wings encircled Oreithyia
> Who was all terror as he caught her up
> And held her as a lover in his arms.[3]

In the sales catalog of Boucher's effects (1771) there occurs (p. 21) among the list of paintings the following entry: "83. L'enlevement [*sic*] d'Orithye par Borée. Hauteur de cette grisaille peinte sur papier, 13 pouces 6 lignes, largeur 10 pouces." The measurements are almost exactly those of the present draw-

ing, and since Boucher planned to include the subject in his *Les Amours des Dieux,* it is clear that he sketched the composition first in black chalk, then painted a monochrome version or *grisaille* (now lost?) and finally a painting.

The tapestry woven at Beauvais in 1749, while showing marked differences in the composition (fig. 30), must ultimately be based on the drawing depicting this scene. Twenty years later Boucher painted another *Boreas and Oreithyia,* closely following the painting which had served as the design for the tapestry. Correctly identified, the painting dated 1769 was reproduced by Nolhac.[4] It is now at the Kimbell Art Museum, there titled *Zephyrus Transporting Psyche.*[5] However, the Kimbell painting clearly illustrates not the scene in which Zephyrus, "the soft and beneficial wind at whose breath the spring flowers open,"[6] gently lifts the nymph Psyche from her solitary rock,[7] but certainly the story of the violent Boreas, carrying off Oreithyia while her companion nymphs watch in horror. Since the iconography of the Ovidian myths was carefully observed and never varied throughout many centuries,[8] we may safely assume Boucher adhered to the original conception of the theme as depicted in the drawing, the painting, and the tapestry of Boreas and Oreithyia.

1. Badin, p. 61.
2. Ovid, *The Metamorphoses*, trans. H. Gregory, New York, 1958, VI, p. 183.
3. Ovid, *The Metamorphoses*, VI, pp. 183–184.
4. P. de Nolhac, *François Boucher, Premier Peintre du Roi*, Paris, 1907, repr. opposite p. 90.
5. *Kimbell Art Museum, Catalogue of the Collection, 1972*, Fort Worth, 1972, repr. (color) p. 106.
6. *New Larousse Encyclopedia of Mythology*, London, 1972, p. 144.
7. See this catalog, no. 38.
8. See M. D. Henkel, "Illustrierte Ausgaben von Ovids Metamorphosen . . . ," *Vorträge der Bibliothek Warburg*, Berlin, Vorträge 1926-1927, pp. 58-144; Kraus Reprint, 1967.

Fig. 30. After Boucher. *Boreas and Oreithyia* (detail).
Tapestry. Rome, Quirinale Palace

65
The Shepherd Paris
Black and white chalk on gray paper
248 x 203
Initialed, upper right: *B*
Provenance: John S. Newberry
Exhibited: Cambridge, Fogg Art Museum, "Thirty-three French Drawings from the Collection of John S. Newberry," 1960, no. 1; Boston, Museum of Fine Arts, "Fifty-one Watercolors and Drawings from the John S. Newberry Collection," 1962, no. 23; Detroit Institute of Arts, "The John S. Newberry Collection," 1965, repr. p. 15
Lent by The Detroit Institute of Arts, Bequest of John S. Newberry

The figure of the seated shepherd is a study for the shepherd Paris in the painting *The Judgment of Paris,* (fig. 31) formerly in the Heidelbach Collection.[1] Boucher did several versions of this theme; the best known is in the Wallace Collection, dated 1754, a composition which is in many respects similar to the Heidelbach picture but also differs from it in many important ways. When the Heidelbach picture, for which our shepherd is a study, was exhibited in Paris in 1875, the brilliant critic W. Thoré-Burger wrote that it was painted "*par larges plans, comme un Veronèse ou un Tintoret.*"[2] It is this generosity of form combined with a lucidity of expression—traceable to the Italian masters—that distinguishes the Heidelbach from the Wallace picture, and gives one the feeling that the former was painted much earlier, before Boucher had adopted the chic and facile manner of the fifties. And it is because of its kinship with late Renaissance models that the figure of the shepherd Paris, defined with nervous, slashing strokes, achieves total plasticity of form. This is equally true of the other figures in the composition for which studies exist: the drawing of Venus (Albertina) whose outstretched hand can be seen, faintly sketched in at the right of our drawing, as the goddess is about to reach for the apple which Paris holds in his hand.[3] The drawing of Minerva, at the right, more monumental than the drawing for the same figure in the Wallace picture (pl. 71) but much less dynamic, was in the Goncourt Collection.[4]

The story of the Judgment of Paris was one of the most celebrated myths of antiquity. The shepherd Paris, son of Priam, King of Troy, was asked to award the golden apple which bore the inscription "To the fairest" to one of three goddesses: Juno (Hera), Venus (Aphrodite), and Minerva (Pallas Athena). Minerva promised him conquest in war; Juno, a throne, and Venus held forth the gift of Helen of Troy. Our earliest source for the story is Euripides, who lets Helen relate the events that led to the fall of Troy:

> A day came, and this Paris judged beneath the trees three Crowns of Life, three diverse Goddesses. The gift of Pallas was of War, to lead his East in conquering battle and make bleed the hearts of Hellas. Hera held a throne—if majesties he craved—to reign alone from Phrygia to the last realm of the West. And Cypris, if he deemed her loveliest, beyond all heaven, made dreams about my face and for her grace gave me. And, lo! her grace was judged the fairest, and she stood above those twain.[5]

1. Sale, Paris, Dec. 16, 1933, no. 16, repr.

2. When the painting was exhibited chez Cadart et Luquet, the catalog, with engravings by A. Martial (1828-1883), was written by W. Thoré-Burger.

3. Repr. by J. Schönbrunner and J. Meder, *Handzeichnungen alter Meister aus der Albertina und anderen Sammlungen*, II, Vienna, 1897, pl. 161.

4. Goncourt Sale, Paris, Feb. 15-17, 1897, no. 20, repr.

5. Euripides, *The Trojan Women*, trans. G. Murray, London, 1931, p. 175.

Fig. 31. *The Judgment of Paris.* Painting. Formerly Heidelbach Collection

66

A Nymph: Study for Apollo and Issé

Red, black and white chalk
320 x 450
Provenance: David-Weill; Barbara Hutton; John Goelet
Bibliography: Société de Reproduction des Dessins de Maîtres,
Paris, 1913, V, repr.; *La Collection David-Weill,* III,
Paris, 1928, pp. 29–30, repr. p. 31 (notes by G. Henriot); B.
Lossky, "L'Appolon et Issé dans l'Oeuvre de François
Boucher," *Gazette des Beaux-Arts,* Nov. 1954, p. 238, fig. 2
Exhibited: New York, Wildenstein, "French Eighteenth
Century Pastels, Watercolors and Drawings from the
David-Weill Collection," 1938, no. 53
Lent by The Art Institute of Chicago, The Joseph and
Helen Regenstein Collection

Fig. 32. *Apollo and Issé.*
Painting. Tours, Musée des
Beaux-Arts

This group of the nymph beside an urn, being embraced by a
sister nymph, merely indicated by a pair of arms, is a study for
the group in the left foreground of the painting *Apollo and
Issé* in the Musée des Beaux-Arts, Tours (fig. 32). The painting,
which is dated 1750, shows the sun god Apollo revealing his
divinity to the nymph Issé. The figure of the reclining nymph
is delicately modeled and defined by a few outline strokes; it
becomes a subtle and complex arabesque when subordinated to
the grand design of the painted composition. While it is surely
not a drawing done for its own sake but a carefully studied
detail, it is also one of the most beautiful nudes by Boucher, with
a vivid, palpitating life of its own.

67
The Adoration of the Shepherds
Black chalk heightened with white and bistre wash on
gray paper
237 x 291
Provenance: Marquis de Chennevières (Lugt, no. 2072; sale,
Paris, May 5–6, 1898, no. 19); Marius Paulme (Lugt 1910;
sale, Paris, May 13, 1929, no. 18, pl. 13); Hon. Irwin
Laughlin
Bibliography: Michel, no. 759; C. Jeanneret, "L'Adoration des
Bergers de François Boucher," *Bulletin de la Société de
l'Histoire de l'Art Français,* 1932, pp. 75–83; Ananoff, no.
628, fig. 110
Exhibited: Washington, National Gallery of Art, 1967
Lent by Rear Admiral and Mrs. Hubert Chanler

When Madame de Pompadour ordered from Boucher an altarpiece for the chapel in her Château de Bellevue, he took endless
pains to carry out the commission, sketching the theme, an
Adoration, many times before exhibiting the finished painting
in the Salon of 1750. Boucher painted and drew some twenty
variations on this theme, borrowing freely from Italian sources—
Guido Reni, Lodovico Carracci, Cavedone, Lanfranco and other
baroque artists. In each of these designs, some done in red or
black chalk, others in pen and ink still others in oil, Boucher
was seeking a new approach to the task he had set himself: to
create a devotional picture in the manner of the Italian baroque.
One of the projects for this *Adoration,* painted in *grisaille,* remained in Boucher's studio until his death; another belonged
to his son-in-law Baudoin; still another, an oil sketch on paper,
was owned by the Goncourts who prized it greatly. The famous
collector Mariette also owned a version which, he was careful
to point out, was after a painting by Cavedone. It is to this group
that the Chanler *Adoration of the Shepherds* belongs.

The definitive version of the Bellevue *Adoration* (engraved
by Fessard as *La Lumière du Monde* and dedicated to Madame
de Pompadour) differs in many respects from the Chanler *Adoration;* the former is an upright composition, the latter horizontal; the Bellevue altarpiece is actually a *Nativity* while the Chanler drawing and its many variants show the shepherds bearing
their humble gifts and prostrating themselves before the Virgin
and Child in the manger.

Before the Château de Bellevue was destroyed during the
Revolution, the *Adoration* altarpiece was removed from the
chapel, but it disappeared completely after 1864. A number of

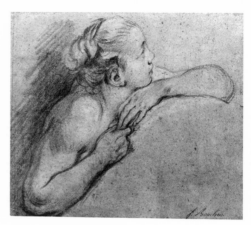

Fig. 34. *Study for Naiad.*
Drawing. Rotterdam, Museum
Boymans-van Beuningen

Fig. 33. *The Rising of the Sun.*
Painting. London, Wallace Collection,
Courtesy of the Trustees

versions, claiming to be the lost original, turned up from time to time, but these were obviously copies, done after the Fessard engraving. In 1932, the French scholar Carlo Jeanneret discovered what he believed to be the lost Bellevue *Adoration*. On the basis of an exhaustive study of all extant paintings, drawings and sketches, he asserted: "Cette *Adoration* est sans doute le tableau capital pour lequel les dessins, les croquis et les esquisses n'auraient servi que de préparations." The painting is today in the Musée des Beaux-Arts, Lyon. Like the Chanler drawing and all the related compositions of the *Adoration,* it carries considerable emotional appeal in its tender portrayal of the scene, without affording the profound religious experience which Boucher had no doubt hoped to arouse in the spectator.

68

Apollo

Black and white chalk on greenish gray paper
543 x 365
Signed at the lower right: *f. Boucher.* Stamped in black ink at
lower left: *ECOLE ACCADEMIQUE DE DESSIN
D.ORLEANS* in circular stamp within which is the number
49; below, the number 34
Provenance: Ecole Académique de Dessin, Orléans; Ryaux
Bibliography: Slatkin, 1967, p. 56.
Exhibited: Paris, Charpentier, "Figures Nues d'Ecole
Française," 1953, no. 20; Minneapolis Institute of Arts,
"Drawings, Paintings and Sculpture from Three Private
Collections," 1960, no. 9; Daniels Collection, 1968, no. 22,
repr.
Lent by David Daniels

The figure of Apollo in one of Boucher's most ambitious compositions, *The Rising of the Sun* (fig. 33, Wallace Collection) is undoubtedly the most beautiful male nude he painted. The drawing of *Apollo,* which served as a study for it, must have been highly regarded in the eighteenth century, for it was acquired by the Academy of Drawing at Orléans to serve as a model for the students. Boucher made frequent trips to Orléans (making landscape sketches of the surrounding countryside) and he may have been invited to give a life class to the students at the Academy there. The drawing of Apollo certainly has the appearance of a study from life, done after a model who was posed in the studio in an attitude reminiscent of the *Apollo Belvedere. The Rising of the Sun,* dated 1753, was one of a pair intended as designs for the Gobelins tapestry works. They were acquired by Madame de Pompadour and exhibited in the Salon of 1753. There can be little doubt that these were the paintings seen by Sir Joshua Reynolds when he visited Boucher in his atelier in Paris in 1752. It must be assumed that the criticism voiced by Reynolds that Boucher painted without the use of models, was without foundation, for there are life studies for almost all the figures in both *The Rising of the Sun* and *The Setting of the Sun:* the studies for the tritons (pls. 69, 70); the naiad at the extreme left in *The Rising of the Sun* (fig. 34) in the Boymans Museum; the nymph in the right foreground, with her back turned, in the Museum at Lille (fig. 35); a preparatory

Fig. 35. *Study for Nymph*.
Drawing. Lille, Musée des Beaux-Arts

Fig. 36. *Two Nymphs and Triton*.
Drawing. Paris, Musée du Louvre

Fig. 37. *Study for Triton*.
Drawing. Weimar, Staatliche
Kunstsammlungen

red chalk drawing in the Louvre based on the life studies of
the two nymphs and the triton in the right foreground (fig. 36).
Boucher's drawing of Apollo was engraved by Louis-Marin
Bonnet as *Académie d'Homme*.[1] As for life studies for the companion painting, *The Setting of the Sun,* they include the reclining nymph in the foreground in the Chanler Collection, and
the nymph at the extreme right, in the Louvre.

1. Cf. Slatkin, 1972, p. 266, figs. 3, 4.

69
A Triton
Black and white chalk with touches of red and *estompe*
220 x 270
Provenance: Charles-Emile Picard
Lent by the Art Institute of Chicago, Joseph and
Helen Regenstein Collection

"Around the chariot of Amphitrite, who was escorted by the gracious Nereids, frisked strange creatures, half-men, half-fish, whose bodies were covered with scales, whose teeth were sharp and whose fingers were armed with claws. Their breast and belly were supplied with fins, and instead of legs they had the forked tail of a marine monster. This lascivious troop played among the waves, noisily blowing on conch shells. They were the Tritons . . . These marine genii took their name from a primitive god, son of Poseidon and Amphitrite, whose name was Triton."[1] Tritons abound in Boucher's great mythological cycles—the *Birth of Venus, Neptune and Amymone, The Rising of the Sun* and *The Setting of the Sun, The Triumph of Amphitrite*—but instead of the ferocious sea monsters of Greek mythology they are male nudes, often quite handsome, posed in the studio in bold but conventional attitudes, their rippling muscles and shaggy hair the only indication of their savage nature.

The triton holding a huge conch shell in the extreme right foreground of Boucher's imposing canvas *The Rising of the Sun* (fig. 33, Wallace Collection) is based on the Chicago *Triton*. Several other drawings, obviously studies from life, served as preparatory sketches for the figures of tritons in *The Rising of the Sun* and *The Setting of the Sun*: the group of two naiads and a triton (fig. 36, Louvre), the triton being the same figure in the Chicago drawing; the triton holding a large flat shell in the Library of the Wallace Collection; the triton resting his chin on his clenched fist in the Cross Collection (pl. 70); the half-length figure of a triton with arms outstretched, holding a scalloped shell, in the Weimar Museum (fig. 37).

1. *Larousse Encyclopedia of Mythology,* Introduction by R. Graves, New York, 1959, p. 169.

70
A Triton
Black chalk on buff paper
196 x 230
Provenance: Charles Gasc (Lugt 542)
Bibliography: Ananoff, no. 904, fig. 155
Lent by Page Cross

This drawing is a study for the figure of the triton at the extreme left in *The Setting of the Sun* which was painted in 1753 and is now in the Wallace Collection, London.

The original Triton, Poseidon's son, was capable of using his primitive energies for good: he guided the Argonauts upon their departure from the golden Hesperides and the blowing of his conch trumpet recalled the deluge with which, according to Ovid, Jupiter had punished the original, vicious race of humans. But the triton, as Wordsworth invoked him in his well-known sonnet, retains from his deep-sea haunts a raw tang of nature, the sublime and untamed:

> Great God! I'd rather be
> A Pagan suckled in a creed outworn;
> So might I, standing on this pleasant lea,
> Have glimpses that would make me less forlorn;
> Have sight of Proteus rising from the sea;
> Or hear old Triton blow his wreathed horn.

71
Study for Minerva

Black chalk heightened with white on buff paper
350 x 192
Inscribed, bottom right: *f. Boucher*
Provenance: Franz Pokorny (Lugt 2036)
Bibliography: Shoolman and Slatkin, p. 62, pl. 35; *Handbook
of the Collections,* California Palace of the Legion of Honor,
1960, repr. p. 61
Exhibited: Sarasota, Ringling Museum, "Master Drawings,"
1967; London, Royal Academy, 1968, no. 97, fig. 144
Lent by the Achenbach Foundation for Graphic Arts,
California Palace of the Legion of Honor

Fig. 38. *The Judgment of Paris*
(detail).
Painting. London, Wallace Collection,
Courtesy of the Trustees

This powerful study of a female nude served as the figure of the
goddess Minerva in one of Boucher's most spectacular compositions, *The Judgment of Paris* (fig. 38). One of four paintings
describing the loves of Venus—*The Visit of Venus to Vulcan,
Cupid and Captive, Venus and Mars Surprised by Vulcan* and
The Judgment of Paris—this last composition on a theme that
has engaged the interests of artists from Rubens to Renoir, tells
of the shepherd Paris, a prince of Troy, who was chosen to
award the golden apple to the fairest of three goddesses: Venus,
Juno and Minerva. In the painting, Paris, seated in the left foreground, is about to hand the apple to Venus while Juno gazes
down angrily from the clouds and Minerva, her back turned
disdainfully to the hapless mortal, floats off into the distance.
The paintings, now in the Wallace Collection, were done by
Boucher in 1754, possibly as a *décor* for the boudoir of Madame
de Pompadour in the Hôtel de l'Arsenal. The study for the
figure of Minerva is one more instance of Boucher's careful
preparation, mainly through sketches from life, for the elaborate
compositions he was to execute.

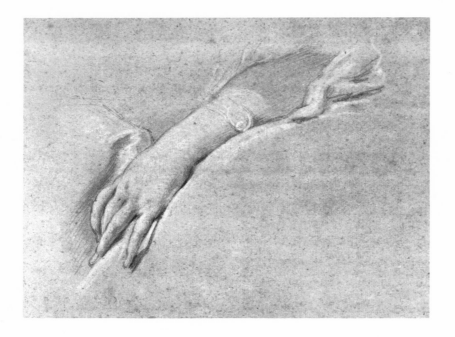

72
Study of a Hand
Black chalk and slight touches of red chalk heightened with
white on light brown paper
221 x 300
Bibliography: Boucher, 1957, ment. under no. 29
Lent by The Metropolitan Museum of Art, Rogers Fund

73
Study of a Hand
Black and white chalk and pencil
220 x 290
Inscribed, lower left: *f. Boucher,* in archaic hand, with
paraphe
Bibliography: Boucher, 1957, no. 29, pl. 29
Lent by Carole Slatkin

Unlike his colleague, the portraitist Maurice-Quentin de La Tour
(1704–88) who, as Michael Levey puts it, "was at his best in
concentrating on the face alone: the face as an expressive, palpitating mask,"[1] Boucher was unable to convey his sitters' character
nor was he able to demonstrate any psychological insight into
their personality. He would rely on background, setting and
accoutrements to build up the image he wished to project, and
fill his canvas with objects symbolizing their status, occupation
or preoccupation to document his knowledge of the person portrayed. Portraits of noble patrons were formal, opulent, almost
impersonal; faces devoid of expression. Only the hands were
alive, revealing some facets of the sitter's character in subtle,
understated language.

This is especially true of the many portraits Boucher did of
his great patron, Madame de Pompadour. He painted her standing beside a spinet, her hand on the keyboard, denoting her
interest in music (Louvre); leaning against the pedestal of a
sculpture, her fan pointing to her favorite spaniel (Wallace Collection); seated in a park-like setting, amid a profusion of roses
(Victoria and Albert Museum), and in her boudoir, surrounded
by exquisite furnishings. Her pose is always regal in its formality,
her face ageless and blank, her hands delicately expressive.

In the Salon of 1757 Boucher exhibited a portrait of Madame
de Pompadour (*Livret,* 1757, no. 12) which showed the marquise in a lavish gown adorned with ribbons, laces and flowers.

In this painting, now in the Alte Pinakothek, Munich,[2] (fig. 39), the *maîtresse en titre* is seated "in the lazy pose suited to a *chaise-longue* . . . her right arm leaning on a cushion of flowered silk; her left arm languidly supports the book in her lap."[3] Actually, it is with her left arm that the marquise leans on the cushion covered in striped, flowered silk, and it is her right hand which holds the open book. The two studies show her left hand (pl. 72), its wrist encircled by a pearl bracelet, and her right hand (pl. 73), with forefinger pressed against a page of the book. (To correspond with the painting, the drawings should be viewed upright.)

While in the painting the hands are slightly plump and dimpled, in the drawings they have a delicate, finely structured quality, supple yet firm. Far better than the face, they express the character of this remarkable woman.

The signature and *paraphe* which appear on the drawing of the right hand (pl. 73) are identical with those discussed in previous entries. The drawings can be dated 1756; although the painting was shown in the Salon of 1757, the date 1756 appears on the little table beside the marquise.

Fig. 39. *Madame de Pompadour.* Painting. Munich, Alte Pinakothek, Bayerische Hypotheken-und Wechsel-Bank Collection

1. Levey, p. 130.
2. For a discussion of the Munich portrait and the other versions, see J. G. Prinz von Hohenzollern, "Die Porträts der Marquise de Baglion und der Marquise de Pompadour," *Pantheon,* July-Aug. 1972, pp. 301-312.
3. Goncourt, p. 158.

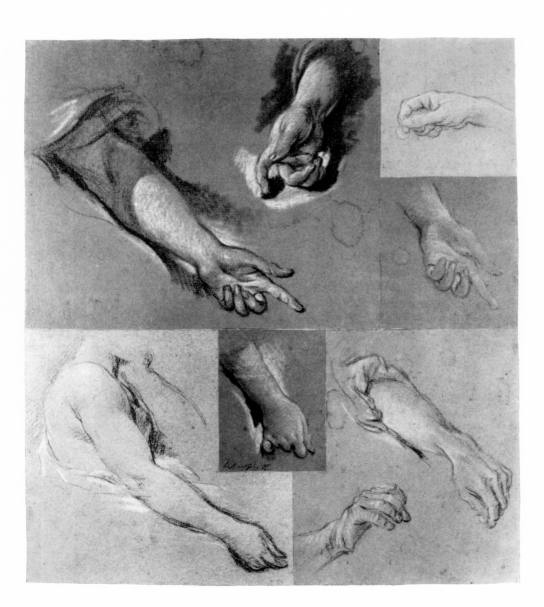

74
Studies of Hands

Red, black and white chalk on tan antique laid paper of different shades; piece at lower left on blue antique laid paper
390 X 337
Center drawing inscribed in archaic hand *f. Boucher* with *paraphe* added. Blind stamp FR (Lugt 1042), lower right
Provenance: Deshayes de Colleville (sale, Paris, Mar. 26, 1765, no. 95)
Exhibited: Cambridge, Fogg Art Museum, "*Studies and Study Sheets,*" 1964, no. 3, repr.; Daniels Collection, 1968, no. 21, repr.
Lent by David Daniels

Livres d'études containing studies of hands, feet and other parts of the human body were constantly used by artists in the seventeenth and eighteenth century. Bloemaert's *Tekenboek* with its several sections devoted to studies of hands and feet, went through several editions, one of which was owned by Boucher (no. 612 in the Boucher *vente*) and the many study sheets of hands by Portail, Carle van Loo and other eighteenth century French artists are undoubtedly based on Bloemaert models. Although Boucher also made use of the *Livre d'études* by Bloemaert, it was not for the purpose of consulting his anatomical models, for he preferred to draw the human figure from life, and to base his painted compositions on drawings and sketches *d'après nature*.

Boucher's manner of drawing hands and feet, fingers and toes, is so unmistakably his that it can almost be used as a test for the authenticity of his work. Women's hands are soft and supple, often dimpled without being flabby, with long tapering fingers and well-defined finger-nails. Men's hands are angular, done in slashing strokes with bold accents denoting their physical strength.

The composite sheet showing hands in various positions undoubtedly comes from the collection of Boucher's son-in-law, Deshayes, whose sale catalog (Mar. 26, 1765) contains, under no. 95, the following entry: "Cinquante études de mains, bras, jambes et pieds, les unes à la pierre noire, les autres à la sanguine. Tous les dessins sous le numéro 94–148 sont originaux de M. Boucher. Grand nombre sont collés." The center sheet bears the same signature with the archaic *h* and the same *paraphe* on the study for the right hand of Madame de Pompadour. Boucher's mat maker who mounted the irregularly shaped drawings on one sheet affixed his blind stamp FR to the mount.

75
Venus with a Dove

Red, black and white chalk on buff paper
276 x 380
Signed, lower left: *F. Boucher 1757*
Provenance: Anonymous sale, Paris, Apr. 1, 1776, no. 80, with
marginal illustration by Gabriel de Saint-Aubin, as *"Une
Femme couchée";* Anonymous sale, Paris, Feb. 19, 1869, as
"Vénus mollement étendue et tenant une Colombe";
Charles Ephrussi
Bibliography: Michel, no. 632, as *"Vénus étendue et tenant
une colombe";* Popham and Fenwick, p. 127, no. 222, repr.;
Ananoff, no. 771; Slatkin, 1972, p. 264 ff., pl. 30
Exhibited: Boucher, 1957, no. 1, repr. on cover; Ottawa,
National Gallery of Canada, "Master Drawings," 1967, no.
36; Toronto, Art Gallery of Ontario, "Master Drawings from
the Collection of the National Gallery of Canada," 1968,
no. 36, pl. 36
Lent by The National Gallery of Canada

The drawing of Venus with a dove was engraved by Louis
Marin Bonnet in 1769 with the title *Le Réveil de Vénus.* A number of copies of this attractive drawing exist, including one by
Bonnet or one of his assistants, but comparison indicates clearly
that the Ottawa drawing is the only version from Boucher's own
hand. The relation of the drawing to the various copies and
to the engraving are fully discussed in the 1972 article by Slatkin
cited above.

76
Danae Receiving the Golden Shower

Red and black chalk, heightened with white on buff paper
311 x 475
Signed (inscribed?) lower left: *f. Boucher 1757*
Provenance: de Montullé (sale, Paris, Dec. 22–30, 1783, under no. 112 [?]); Marquis de Cypierre (sale, Paris, Mar. 10, 1845, no. 174 [?]); Etienne Arago (sale, Paris, Feb. 8, 1872 [?]); Ludwig Neumann; Samuel H. Kress Collection
Bibliography: Michel, no. 470(?); Ananoff, no. 732; Slatkin, 1972, pp. 271, 273–276, pl. 36
Exhibited: Washington, National Gallery of Art, "Drawings from the Collection of the National Gallery of Art," 1966; New York, Knoedler, "Masters of the Loaded Brush," 1967, no. 63, pl. 63a; London, Royal Academy, 1968, no. 96, fig. 143
Lent by the National Gallery of Art, Samuel H. Kress Collection

This very handsome drawing, of which another version exists (formerly Guyot de Villeneuve Collection) was engraved by Louis-Marin Bonnet with the title *Vénus sur les nuées retenant une colombe*. The Kress drawing may possibly be a copy by Bonnet or one of his assistants in preparation for the engraving. The relationship of the drawing to the Villeneuve version, the oil sketch in the Nationalmuseum, Stockholm, and the Bonnet engraving is discussed in the 1972 article by Slatkin cited above.

77
Cupids as Sculptors

Pen and bistre wash
Oval, 215 x 153
Glomy stamp G, bottom center (Lugt 1119)
Provenance: A. Alferoff; Charkow University and Museum—
The Hermitage (sale, Leipzig, Apr. 29, 1931, no. 33)
Exhibited: Boucher, 1957, no. 13, pl. XI
Lent by Mr. and Mrs. Lenard M. Shavick

The group of cupids sculpting a bust of a little girl occurs in a number of compositions which Boucher did in the 1750s. A painting in the Anthony de Rothschild Collection at Ascott, dated 1758, utilizes this motif, as does the much larger picture, *Les Génies des arts* in the Musée de Peinture et Sculpture, Angers. The sculptured bust of the child appears to be taken from an existing work by Jacques Saly (1717–1776) which was greatly admired and copied in his day.[1] The child is thought by some scholars to represent the daughter of Madame de Pompadour, Alexandrine d'Etiolles, who died very young, and by others, the daughter of Jean-François de Troy (1679–1752), head of the French Academy in Rome. Michael Levey, who has, quite plausibly, assumed the latter to be true, writes: "Though it has been common to think of the child portrayed as Madame de Pompadour's short-lived daughter, it is more subtle, if less glamorous, to recall that she is quite likely to be the recently widowed de Troy's sole surviving child, who herself never reached adulthood."[2] Despite Mr. Levey's convincing arguments, it is nevertheless difficult to explain Boucher's persistent use of the motif unless the child, whose portrait bust was done by Saly, was of special significance. Even in this rapid sketch, the distinct personality of the child, as Saly saw her, is conveyed by Boucher's brush: "It is the portrait of a child in which truth comes before prettiness . . . the downcast eyes and the closed mouth which convey a touching sensation of the withdrawn."[3]

1. About a dozen replicas of Saly's *Bust of a Young Girl* are extant, among them a bronze in the Widener Collection at the National Gallery of Art; marble busts at the Victoria and Albert Museum, the Glyptothek in Copenhagen; The Hermitage and the David-Weill Collection, Neuilly, as well as terra-cotta and plaster models. Michael Levey believes that the Victoria and Albert bust may be Saly's original, but Peter Marlow prefers to think that it is the David-Weill marble.

2. M. Levey, p. 82. A full discussion of Saly's sculpture of the unknown little girl is to be found in M. Levey, "A New Identity for Saly's *'Bust of a Young Girl,'*" *Burlington Magazine*, Feb. 1965, p. 91.

3. Levey, p. 82.

Two Nudes: Study for Pan and Syrinx
Black chalk heightened with white on buff paper
253 x 397
Inscribed, lower left, in eighteenth century hand:
f. Boucher, with *paraphe*
Provenance: Mrs. W. H. Crocker
Bibliography: Quarterly Bulletin, San Francisco Museum of
Art, Oct.-Dec. 1939, repr. p. 21; Shoolman and Slatkin, p. 66,
pl. 37
Exhibited: Oakland, Mills College, "Old Master Drawings,"
1937, no. 6
Lent anonymously

Fig. 40. *Pan and Syrinx.*
Painting. London, The National
Gallery, Courtesy of the Trustees

The theme of Pan and Syrinx had interested Boucher for some time, and he had done several ink sketches of the subject, but it was not until 1759 that he gave final expression to it in the painting now in the National Gallery, London (fig. 40). The drawing of Syrinx and her sister nymph is a preliminary study for the painting, but while the figure of the nymph reclining, with her back turned, remains essentially the same, the figure of Syrinx, fleeing in terror from Pan, has been considerably altered to produce a more dynamic composition. Another study for the painting is discussed in the following entry.

This study of the two nymphs also bears the artist's name in archaic script, with the additional *paraphe* or flourish, having undoubtedly formed part of the same group as the *Four Heads of Cherubs* (pl. 8), and the other drawings which are signed and marked in the same manner.

79
The Nymph Syrinx

Red, black and white chalk on prepared beige paper
202 x 292
Provenance: Comte de la Béraudière; Earl of Carnarvon;
Marquess of Dufferin and Ava
Lent by the Indiana University Art Museum, Evan F. Lilly
Memorial

Study for the figure of Syrinx in the painting *Pan and Syrinx,*
National Gallery, London (fig. 40). This highly finished drawing corresponds much more closely to the central figure in the
painting, than does the sketchier version of Syrinx and her sister
nymph (pl. 78), which undoubtedly preceded it. In the Indiana
drawing, the gesture of fright and the contorted limbs of the
terrified Syrinx convey more precisely the image in Ovid's version of the legend, according to which Syrinx fled into the arms
of a sister nymph to escape from Pan.

> In the chill mountains of Arcadia there lived a nymph,
> the most famous of all the wood nymphs of Nonacris.
> The other nymphs called her Syrinx. Many a time she
> had eluded the pursuit of satyrs and of other spirits
> who haunt the shady woodlands or the fertile fields.
> She was a follower of the Ortygian goddess, imitating
> her in her pastimes, and in her virtue too. As she was
> returning from Mount Lycaeus, Pan caught sight of her,
> Pan who wears on his head a wreath of sharp-leaved
> pine . . . she, scorning his prayers, ran off through the
> pathless forest till she came to the still waters of the
> sandy Ladon. When the river halted her flight, she
> prayed her sisters of the stream to transform her; and
> when Pan thought he had at last caught hold of Syrinx,
> he found that instead of the nymph's body he held a
> handful of marsh reeds. As he stood sighing, the wind
> blew through the reeds, and produced a thin plaintive
> sound.

It was from these reeds that Pan fashioned his flute, called
a Syrinx.[1]

1. Ovid, *Metamorphoses,* I, 689-712. Trans. M. Innes, London, 1971,
pp. 47-48.

80

Design for the Frontispiece of Corneille's Rodogune

Black chalk heightened with white on blue paper
Two drawings mounted together, the left drawing
300 x 214; the right drawing 304 x 214
The left drawing signed, lower left: *f. Boucher f*
Provenance: J. B. de Graef (Lugt 1120); E. Wauters
(Lugt 911; sale, Amsterdam, June 15–16, 1926, no. 28)
Bibliography: Portalis, II, p. 522; F. Lees, *The Art of the*
Great Masters, London, 1913, p. 151, figs. 171, 172; P.
Gusman, "Madame de Pompadour, Artiste et graveur,"
Byblis, 1926, pp. 27, 28; *A Review of the Growth . . . between*
. . . 1924 . . . and . . . 1929, New York, The Pierpont Morgan
Library, 1930, pp. 41, 110; P. Grigaut, "Madame de
Pompadour and the *Rodogune* Frontispiece," *Art Quarterly,*
Summer 1948, p. 269, fig. 3; Jean-Richard, pp. 92, 93
Lent by The Pierpont Morgan Library

In 1759 Boucher designed the frontispiece for Pierre Corneille's tragedy *Rodogune* which was printed, at Madame de Pompadour's request, in her apartments at Versailles. The two drawings in the Morgan Library are preliminary studies for the illustration of Scene IV, Act V, of the tragedy. A drawing in pen and ink for this frontispiece, showing the entire scene, was in the collection of Baron Henri de Rothschild; the print, which closely follows it, was, according to its legend, etched by Madame de Pompadour and retouched by Cochin. A rare proof of the etching (fig. 41) indicated, according to Paul Grigaut, that Boucher had, in fact, etched the plate himself and gallantly allowed the marquise to sign her name to the plate.

The tragic story of Rodogune, Princess of Parthia, and Cleopatra, Queen of Syria, was Corneille's favorite play. He makes of Cleopatra one of the most evil characters on the stage (yet one who arouses our pity), a woman who in jealous fury murders her husband the king, who wanted to set her aside in order to marry Rodogune. Cleopatra's twin sons also love Rodogune. Determined to prevent either of them from marrying the Parthian, Cleopatra first slays one son, then tries to destroy the other by offering him a chalice of poisoned wine. The Parthian princess accuses the queen of murder, and Cleopatra in turn attempts to fasten the blame on Rodogune.

The scene depicted in Boucher's drawing is the moment when Rodogune points to the guilty queen who in self-loathing lifts the goblet to her own lips and drinks the poisoned wine.

"Seigneur," cries Rodogune, *"voyez ses yeux déjà tous égarés, troublés et furieux."* ("My lord, see her eyes, dazed and wild.") In the Morgan Library drawing, the left side of the composition represents Cleopatra, Queen of Syria, attended by her lady-in-waiting Laonice; the right side depicts the Parthian princess Rodogune and Antiochus, son of Cleopatra and heir to the throne of Syria. In the etched frontispiece, the focus is on the central figure of Cleopatra, the evil and tragic heroine of the play, and it is interesting to recall Corneille's explanation regarding the title of the play: that he would have called it *Cleopatra, "sur qui tombe toute l'action tragique"* (on whom all the tragic action rests), had he not feared that the public would confuse the Syrian queen with that last, famous queen of Egypt who bore the same name. Boucher's preliminary drawings do not show, as the finished drawing does, the columned palace hall which served as the stage set.

A drawing in black chalk of the queen and her attendant, much more sketchily done than the Morgan Library drawings, was in the Jourdeuil Collection (Lugt 527) and recently passed through Christie's (Nov. 26, 1968, no. 131). A red chalk drawing of the same subject is cataloged by Michel (no. 2624); and a pen drawing heightened with Chinese white, was in the Mühlbacher Sale (1899, no. 90) where it was listed as *Rodogune. Scène à six personnages de la tragédie de Corneille. Illustration unique d'une édition publiée par Mme de Pompadour, en 1760.*[1] This was probably a preliminary sketch for the drawing in the Morgan Library.

Aside from the literary interest attached to it, the drawing for the *Rodogune* frontispiece is noteworthy for its restraint of line, almost neo-classical in feeling.

1. Also in the du Sartel Sale, 1894; see Michel, no. 2615.

Fig. 41. Frontispiece to *Rodogune*. Etching-engraving. Mr. and Mrs. Walter M. Spink Collection

81
Woman in Classical Dress

Black chalk heightened with white on buff paper
350 x 225
Provenance: Groult (sale, Paris, June 21–22, 1920, no. 130);
C. R. Rudolf (sale, London, Sotheby's, May 21, 1963, no. 50,
repr.)
Bibliography: Ananoff, no. 755
Exhibited: London, Royal Academy of Arts, "Drawings by
Old Masters," 1953, no. 428; London, The Arts Council
Gallery, Birmingham, City Museum & Art Gallery, Leeds,
City Art Gallery, "Old Master Drawings from the Collection
of Mr. C. R. Rudolf," 1962, no. 166, pl. 26
Lent anonymously

The figure of the young woman with grave mien, standing beside an antique pedestal, has not heretofore been associated with Boucher's design for the frontispiece of Corneille's play *Rodogune,* but comparison with the figures in that composition leads to the conjecture that this might indeed be another study for the figure of the Parthian princess. The style of dress is similar; a loose, flowing robe over which a richly embroidered mantle is draped, and for a headdress, a veil worn turbanwise, falling over the shoulder, almost to the waist. Boucher does not differentiate between the costume worn by the Parthian princess and that worn by the Syrian queen or her attendant, so that our drawing might have been a study which he tried out for the figure of Laonice.

82
Tête à Tête

Black chalk heightened with white on buff paper
333 x 230
Signed and dated at left on wall: *F. Boucher 1764*
Provenance: de Stainville; Chalandray; Marquis de Cypierre
(sale, Paris, Mar. 10, 1845, no. 189); Marquis de Montesquiou-
Fezensac (sale, Paris, Mar. 19, 1897, no. 2); Baron Vittat;
Joseph E. Widener
Bibliography: Leymarie, no. 486; H. Comstock, "Master
Drawings in San Francisco," *Connoisseur,* Sept., 1940, p. 115,
repr. p. 113; Shoolman and Slatkin, no. 38, repr; Ananoff, no.
248, fig. 49; P. H. Hulton, "France in the Eighteenth Century
at the Royal Academy," *Master Drawings, 6,* no. 2, 1968, p. 166
Exhibited: New London, Conn., Lyman Allyn Museum,
"Drawings," 1936, no. 95; San Francisco, 1940, no. 7;
Montreal Museum of Fine Arts, "The Eighteenth Century
Art of France and England," 1950, no. 68; Philadelphia
Museum of Art, "Masterpieces of Drawing," 1950–1951, no. 7;
Richmond, Virginia Museum of Fine Arts, *"Les Fêtes
Galantes,"* 1956; Paris, Orangerie, 1958, no. 35, pl. 41; Los
Angeles, U.C.L.A., "French Masters, Rococo to Romanticism,"
1961, no. 27; repr.; London, Royal Academy, 1968, no. 95, fig. 142
Lent by the National Gallery of Art, Washington, Widener Collection

Boucher's *Et in Arcadia ego* is a land where pretty shepherdesses, barefoot and beribboned, are forever courted by faithful shepherds against a background of luxurious foliage and half-ruined fountains. There are only the faintest echoes of Theocritus, Vergil or Honoré d'Urfé, and no poetic discourses on bucolic life, for these are set conventional themes on which Boucher played endless variations. He painted and drew some five hundred pastorales which were repeated, endlessly, on fans and snuff boxes, porcelains and tapestries, screens and furniture, performing a purely decorative function. Often a lyrical element would emerge, as in the charming *Tête à Tête,* recalling the raison d'être of these painted eclogues—to contrast an artificial, convention-bound court and city life with the idyllic life of the shepherds among natural surroundings.

The drawing *Tête à Tête* was engraved by Demarteau with certain variations (Leymarie, no. 62) and copied a number of times by imitators of Boucher's style. One of Boucher's favorite subjects, the young shepherd and his love are shown again in a very similar composition, a painting in the Collection Bentinck-Thyssen-Bornemisza (Royal Academy, 1968, fig. 119). The Washington drawing is dated 1764; the Thyssen painting bears the date 1766.

83
Allegory of Music

Pen and sanguine wash
Oval, 165 x 230
Provenance: L. Coblentz (sale, Paris, Dec. 15–16, 1904,
no. 21)
Bibliography: Michel, no. 993; Ananoff, no. 940
Lent anonymously

Boucher's work enjoyed great popularity in Germany where it was much copied and imitated, especially by former pupils of his (Joseph Herman, Melling, Mänlich, etc.) The engraver Wille did a brisk business in Boucher prints and drawings which he sent from Paris to clients in Germany, but some of the German princes commissioned Boucher directly to do paintings for them. The Elector of Bavaria ordered two paintings from Boucher: an *Allegory of Music* and an *Allegory of Painting.* These paintings, today in the National Gallery of Art, Washington, are dated 1764 and 1765 respectively.

The preliminary drawing in pen and wash for the *Allegory of Music* (fig. 42) suggests that Boucher may have considered an oval format for these two pendants, but decided on horizontal compositions instead. The painting of the *Allegory of Music* follows the preliminary study very closely in the seated figure personifying Music, but the artist has made a number of changes which simplify and strengthen the composition: he has eliminated one of the *amoretti* at right, and substituted a pair of doves beside the open music score. In the drawing, the flute and music score are at the feet of the Muse; a cherub is reaching for them. In the painting, the little cherub holding the laurel wreath hands the ivory flute to the Muse who touches the seven-stringed lyre with her right hand instead of her left. At the extreme left of the painting Boucher had added a helmet and sword (the attributes of Mars, god of war) which lie at the feet of the Muse, half concealed by clouds and drapery. These undoubtedly symbolize the triumph of music over the violence of men. Michel stresses the "vigorous" quality of the drawing which is, indeed, done with uncommon brilliance; more impressive, perhaps, is the fact that this drawing of almost miniature size served as a sketch for two paintings quite grand in scale.

The *Allegory of Music* has been interpreted by one critic as an allusion to Plato's Banquet,[1] while the Muse (perhaps because of the doves) is believed to be Venus, the goddess of love. "Venus

Fig. 42. *Allegory of Music.*
Painting. Washington, National
Gallery of Art, Samuel H. Kress
Collection

is seated near an open music score, her usual attributes beside
her: the roses, the doves, the helmet and sword of Mars. Two
cherubs hand her a flute—an erotic emblem evoking the carnal
Venus, and the seven-stringed lyre whose music is equated with
the harmony of the spheres—an allusion to the celestial Venus.
The goddess gazes at the flute, but places her hand on the lyre:
she has made her choice. Is it not curious to find in this seemingly
galant work of art by a painter reputedly so frivolous, an allusion
to the Banquet of Plato?"

1. A. P. de Mirimonde, "Les allégories de la musique," *Gazette des
Beaux-Arts,* May, 1969, p. 357.

84

Vertumnus and Pomona

Black chalk heightened with white on greenish paper
Oval, 290 x 256
Blind stamp G on eighteenth century mount, bottom right
(Lugt 1119)
Bibliography: T. C. Howe, "*Vertumnus and Pomona* by
François Boucher," *Museum Bulletin,* California Palace of
the Legion of Honor, San Francisco, Mar.-Apr. 1968, p. 6,
fig. 7
Lent by The Hyde Collection

Another episode from Ovid's *Metamorphoses,* and a favorite
subject with artists for centuries, was the legend of Vertumnus
and Pomona, a tale of two ancient Roman divinities, the nymph
Pomona who presided over the fruit of trees, and Vertumnus,
god of orchards.

Pomona was the only nymph who did not love the wild
woodland. She cared for fruits and orchards . . . her de-
light was in pruning and grafting and everything that
belongs to the gardener's art. She shut herself away
from men, alone with her beloved trees, and let no
wooer come near her. Of all that sought her, Vertumnus
was the most ardent, but he could make no headway.
Often he was able to enter her presence in disguise, now
as a rude reaper bringing her a basket of barley-ears,
now as a clumsy herdsman, or a vine pruner. At last . . .
he came to her disguised as a very old woman, so that it
did not seem strange to Pomona when after admiring
her fruit he said to her, 'But you are far more beautiful,'
and kissed her. Still, he kept on kissing her as no old
woman would have done, and Pomona was startled.
Perceiving this, he let her go and sat down opposite an
elm tree over which grew a vine loaded with purple
grapes. 'How lovely they are together, and how different they would be apart, the tree useless and the vine
flat on the ground, unable to bear fruit. Are you not like
such a vine? You turn from all who desire you.'[1]
Pomona at long last yields to his entreaties.

Boucher did a number of versions of this tale; one of these is
the painting in the California Palace of the Legion of Honor
on which a Beauvais tapestry is based (1757). Another is the
painting in the Louvre (fig. 43) of quite a different design,
which served as the basis for a tapestry woven at the Gobelins
manufactory;[2] both the painting and the tapestry are dated

1763. The drawing of Vertumnus and Pomona in The Hyde Collection while differing in some respects from the painting is certainly the study on which the finished composition in the Louvre is based, and may therefore also be dated about 1763.

The tapestries woven at the Gobelins manufactory were all intended for the royal household, or as gifts to other sovereigns or foreign embassies. Boucher would therefore have made a point of changing the composition from the earlier version so as to present a model exclusively for the royal collection. The background, sketchily done in the drawing, is worked out in precise and luxurious detail in the picture: the richly ornamented vase becomes a fountain; the fruit at Pomona's side, barely indicated in the drawing, becomes a glowing still-life; the gourd in the foreground is eliminated to emphasize the beauty of the flower-filled basket in the foreground. There is hardly a better instance of the development of a theme from sketch to painted composition than is afforded by comparison of the drawing from The Hyde Collection with the Louvre painting.

A second drawing on the Vertumnus and Pomona theme is in the collection of Mrs. O'Donnell Hoover (fig. 44).[3] This handsome drawing, an upright composition, was most likely planned as a pendant to the drawing of Pygmalion, also in the Hoover Collection;[4] both these drawings must have been intended as projects for upright panels, such as the painting in the California Palace of the Legion of Honor. Still another version, of almost identical dimensions as the Hoover drawing, but horizontal, was in the Trézel Collection.[5] It would almost seem as though Boucher had tried in every way to find a new formula for a well-worn theme.

Toward the end of his career he was called upon once more to interpret the classic myth of Vertumnus and Pomona, this time as an illustration for the French edition of Ovid's *Metamorphoses* by Abbé Banier (1767–1771). Boucher's illustration for the text was engraved by Augustin de Saint-Aubin.

1. E. Hamilton, *Mythology,* New York, 1957, pp. 285–286.
2. See M. Fenaille, *Etat Général des Tapisseries de la Manufacture des Gobelins. . . .* Paris, 1907, IV, p. 234.
3. Formerly in the Alphonse Trézel Collection (sale, Paris, May 17, 1935, no. 23, repr.).
4. Repr. in the Trézel Sale catalog, no. 24.
5. Also repr. in the Trézel catalog, no. 21.

Fig. 43. *Vertumnus and Pomona.* Painting. Paris, Musée du Louvre

Fig. 44. *Vertumnus and Pomona.* Drawing. Mrs. O'Donnell Hoover Collection

85
Design for the Diploma for the Freemasons of Bordeaux

Brush, gray and cream oil paint, on heavy paper
391 X 270
Inscribed on the banderoles: *POST TENEBRAS LUX
LOGE DE L'AMITIE*
Bibliography: J. Bean, *100 European Drawings in The
Metropolitan Museum of Art,* New York, 1964, no. 58, repr.;
A. H. Mayor, "Practical Fantasies," *Apollo,* Sept. 1965, p. 246,
fig. 9; Jean-Richard, p. 66
Exhibited: New York, The Metropolitan Museum of Art,
"French Drawings and Prints of the Eighteenth Century," 1972, no. 4
Lent by The Metropolitan Museum of Art, Rogers Fund

"This level which we carry with us teaches us to measure men that we may respect their human qualities and not be overawed by wordly honors. The Freemason is a free man, the friend alike of rich and poor, provided they be worthy." Such was the code of that brotherhood of men which spread throughout Europe during the eighteenth century, condemned by the church and forbidden by the governments. "Lodges multiplied," wrote the French scholar Paul Hazard, "and into them flocked notabilities, prosperous citizens, members of the learned professions . . . *Les vrais Amis, La Bonne Amitié, La Parfaite Amitié,* such names were often given to their lodges. No one was more eager than they for that political freedom which was one of the aspirations of the age." POST TENEBRAS LUX (After Darkness, Light), the motto inscribed on the Metropolitan Museum's drawing, links the brotherhood of Freemasons to the *Philosophes* of the eighteenth century, the prime movers of the Age of Enlightenment. Paul Hazard relates that Voltaire himself became a member of the fraternal order; when this most famous of *Philosophes* entered the *Loge de l'Amitié* to receive his diploma, he was excused from the ceremonies of initiation. "Escorted into the hall by a commission of nine delegates who had gone to meet him, he came in, leaning on the arm of Benjamin Franklin."[1] In England, Josiah Wedgwood, James Watts and Erasmus Darwin joined the brotherhood. George Washington and Wolfgang Amadeus Mozart were other illustrious members. "Such men," writes E. J. Hobsbawm, "everywhere flocked into the lodges of Freemasonry, where class distinctions did not count and the ideology of the Enlightenment was propagated with disinterested zeal."[2]

Boucher's drawing, a design for the diploma awarded to members of the Bordeaux Lodge, "does no more," writes Jacob Bean, "than suggest, with brilliant, abbreviated brushwork, the general outlines of the composition and the disposition of light and shade; the task of translating the design into linear terms required by the reproductive process was left to the engraver."[3]

The female figure of Charity surrounded by cherubs symbolizes the beneficence of the Masonic movement, a somewhat paradoxical expression, since women were excluded from the secret society. But the personification of Charity was traditionally female, and so she remained, enthroned above the cartouche, opening her arms to the infant cherubs nestling against her, while other cherubs display the emblematic instruments which can still be observed on the lapels of members of the Brotherhood. Boucher's drawing was engraved by Pierre-Philippe Choffard in 1766; the drawing itself, as indicated on the print, was done a year earlier.[4]

1. P. Hazard, *European Thought in the Eighteenth Century,* trans. J. L. May, New York, 1967, pp. 268-269.

2. E. J. Hobsbawm, *The Age of Revolution,* London, 1961, p. 21.

3. J. Bean, p. 58.

4. M. Roux, *Inventaire du Fonds Français, Graveurs du XVIIIe Siècle,* Paris, 1940, IV, pp. 406-407.

86
Design for a Clock

Black chalk and brush heightened with white on buff paper
318 x 194
Signed and dated on base: *F. Boucher 1765*
Provenance: Baron Nathaniel de Rothschild; Baron
Alphonse de Rothschild
Exhibited: Montreal Museum of Fine Arts, "The Eighteenth
Century Art of France and England," 1950, no. 66;
Boucher, 1957, no. 42, pl. 28; Paris, Orangerie, 1958, no. 36,
pl. 45
Bibliography: Michel, no. 2558
Lent by the S. Kramarsky Trust Fund

It has often been said that the eighteenth century was obsessed with the clock. To measure time with the greatest possible accuracy while simultaneously conveying the flux of time was a problem that preoccupied a whole era, and the talents of some of the best artists in Europe were devoted to the designing and construction of clocks. (One of Boucher's younger contemporaries, the keen-witted Beaumarchais, son of a famous clockmaker, also embarked for a time on the career of *horloger*.) In 1759 Ferdinand Berthoud published a four-volume treatise on the subject: *L'Art de Conduire et de Régler Les Pendules et les Montres* and his *Essai sur L'Horlogerie* went through several editions. But the model for rococo design in clocks was Oppenord's *Livre des Pendules,* engraved by Huquier, a work surely not unknown to Boucher. Gabriel de Saint-Aubin's well-known *Portrait of a Clockmaker* (Wickes Collection, Museum of Fine Arts, Boston) shows such an elaborate clock with swirling figures upholding the intricate mechanism. Boucher also designed clocks for his patrons: one for Lalive de Jully, another most elaborate one for Madame de Pompadour's brother, the Marquis de Marigny. This last design which shows four draped female figures who symbolize the Arts, upholding a globe surmounted by the figures of Time and Love, is now in the Musée des Arts Décoratifs, Paris (fig. 45). Here the clock is a *cadran mobilier,* a globe around which runs a band on which the hours and minutes are marked. All the other designs show the dial in a circular case.

The Goncourts mention (p. 206) a drawing which was probably one of the three clock designs catalogued by Michel (no. 2558), but this cannot have been the Kramarsky drawing, as the Orangerie catalog states, for the Goncourt entry reads: "A la vente de M. de Sireuil passait encore un projet de pendule ornée de deux figures de femmes", while the only entry in the Sireuil catalog (1781), which could have referred to a clock design is no. 134, "Une étude de deux Femmes debout et drapées, dont l'une est vue par le dos, et tient d'une main un médaillon de sculpture; Dessin aux crayons noir et blanc sur papier bleu. Hauteur 13 pouces, largeur 8 pouces." However, the two female figures in the Kramarsky drawing are placed on either side of a clock face, not a sculptured medallion, and the drawing is on buff, not blue paper. A drawing in the Besançon Museum, on faded blue-gray paper, showing the same design with the composition reversed and the two female figures upholding a sculptured medallion with the portrait of Louis XV, does correspond to the entry in the Sireuil catalog.

Fig. 45. *Design for a Clock.*
Drawing. Paris, Musée des Arts
Décoratifs

87
Design for a Funeral Monument
Black chalk heightened with white on blue paper
292 x 178
Signed, lower left: *f.B.* with *paraphe*
Provenance: Anonymous sale, Paris, May 4, 1906, no. 10;
Baron Nathaniel de Rothschild
Bibliography: Goncourt, p. 206
Lent by Arthur L. Liebman

Boucher's drawing of two half-draped female figures leaning, in an attitude of sorrow, against a fluted column beneath which is a medallion portrait of a young woman with classical profile, was intended, as the engraving indicates, to serve as a design for a funeral monument to a young woman, Mademoiselle Sandow of Berlin. It was engraved by the banker Eberts, an amateur printmaker who engraved a number of other drawings by Boucher. The drawing is freely sketched and quite rococo in feeling, with an ornamental vase festooned by a garland held by two cherubs, and two doves crowning the vase. At the base of the monument is a cherub holding an open book (a musical score?) and the trumpet of fame. The engraving is far more severe, almost neo-classical in feeling, with most of the rococo ornamental detail suppressed. The base of the column bears the inscription DIVAE DOR: SANDOW BEROL SACRUM[1] and a dedication to Baron Friesendorff, secretary to the King of Sweden, perhaps the young lady's protector.

1. Sanctuary of the divine Dorothea Sandow of Berlin.

Fig. 46. *The Continence of Scipio.*
Drawing. Quimper, Musée des
Beaux-Arts

88

The Continence of Scipio

Brown and red chalk on buff paper
495 x 301
Bibliography: Slatkin, 1967, p. 62; Bacou, p. 103
Exhibited: Boucher, 1957, no. 22, (as *Judgment of Solomon*),
repr.; Detroit Institute of Arts, "French Drawings and Water
Colors from Michigan Collections," 1962, no. 13, repr.; Detroit
Institute of Arts, "The Institute Collects," 1964–65, p. 18,
repr. p. 6; Toronto, Ottawa, San Francisco, New York,
1972–73, no. 13, pl. 86
Lent by The Detroit Institute of Arts, Laura H. Murphy Fund

Incorrectly identified at first as the *Judgment of Solomon,* this
drawing is one of several sketches which Boucher did for a
composition of *The Continence of Scipio* which he was commissioned to paint. Of the three drawings here exhibited, this would
seem to be the earliest in date, freely and rapidly executed, as
though it had been done in the first flush of the artist's conception of his subject. The medium here employed is simply red
and brown chalk: the other three known drawings for the composition are more elaborately worked out in wash (pl. 89), brush
and brown ink (pl. 90) and even heightened with white (fig. 46).

89

The Continence of Scipio

Brown chalk and brush and brown wash
482 x 284

Provenance: Georges Bourgarel (sale, Paris, Nov. 11–13, 1922,
no. 61; Paul Suzor; Anonymous sale, Paris, Mar. 11, 1964,
no. 41, pl. 1; Anonymous sale, Paris, March 16, 1966, no. 2
Bibliography: Ananoff, no. 1013; fig. 166; *The Metropolitan
Museum of Art Bulletin,* Oct. 1967, pp. 58, 60, repr. p. 60;
Slatkin, 1967, p. 62; Bacou, p. 103; Rosenberg cited under no. 13
Exhibited: New York, The Metropolitan Museum of Art,
"French Drawings and Prints of the Eighteenth Century,"
1972, no. 5
Lent by The Metropolitan Museum of Art
Joseph Pulitzer Bequest

This is another of the projected compositions for the painting
Boucher was commissioned to do on the theme of *The Continence* (sometimes called the *Generosity* or the *Magnanimity*)
of Scipio. After visiting the Salon of 1767, Diderot wrote, "He
could not seem to please his patron despite all the efforts he made,
and he finally gave up and asked that the commission be given
to his pupil Vien."[1]

The story tells of the Roman general Scipio Africanus who,
at the fall of Carthage, was offered as a prize the beautiful bride
of the Celt-Iberian chieftain, Allucius. "She was a young girl and
so beautiful," wrote the historian Livy, "that everyone turned to
look at her wherever she went. Scipio asked where she came
from and who her parents were, and was told amongst other
things that she was betrothed to a Celt-Iberian chieftain, a young
man named Allucius. He at once sent for the girl's parents and
her lover, and as soon as the latter arrived, he spoke to him,
choosing his words with more care than in what he said to the
father and mother, simply because he had learned meanwhile
of the man's passionate love for his betrothed. 'The woman
whom you are to marry was taken prisoner and brought to me
by our soldiers, and I now learn that you care for her deeply—
and indeed her beauty makes it easy to believe that this is so.
Your bride has been treated under my protection with all the
delicacy she would have found in the house of her parents, your
own parents-to-be; she has been kept for you, an inviolate gift.'
Then the parents and relatives of the girl were sent for. They
had brought with them a weight of gold sufficient for her ransom,
and begged Scipio to take the treasure as a gift. Scipio agreed to
take it; then, having asked for it to be laid at his feet, he called
Allucius and told him to take the gold and keep it for his own,
saying, "This is my wedding present, to be added to the dowry
you will receive from your bride's father."[2]

The picture, which was finally painted by Joseph Vien, is in
the Palace of Fontainebleau.

1. J. Seznec and J. Adhémar, *Diderot, Salons,* Oxford, 1963, p. 87,
[trans.]
2. Livy, *The War with Hannibal,* trans. A. de Selincourt, London, 1965,
bk. 26, pp. 421-422.

90
The Continence of Scipio
Brush and brown ink over pencil on buff paper
420 x 264
Provenance: M. G. (sale, Paris, May 30, 1873, no. 10 [?])
Bibliography: Michel, no. 875(?); Ananoff, no. 1011, fig. 165;
Slatkin, 1967, p. 62; Bacou, p. 103; Rosenberg, p. 137, cited
under no. 13
Lent anonymously

It is easy to understand why Boucher made so many attempts to satisfy the patron who had commissioned *The Continence of Scipio,* for the subject had proved a challenge to many artists, including Primaticcio, Veronese, Poussin and Boucher's own teacher François Lemoyne.[1] It was, in fact, a theme made to order for Boucher's brush, for it told a moving and heroic story which allowed the artist to display as central figures a beautiful young woman, richly clad; a young warrior amidst the full panoply of Roman arms and in the foreground, an array of precious objects and luxurious fabrics—all the most attractive studio props. In this version, the winged genii bearing aloft the trumpet of fame and the laurel of victory are omitted, and Allucius has joined hands with his bride.

1. Pigler, II, pp. 404-409.

91

A Captive Brought before an Oriental Ruler

Pen, brown ink and gouache heightened with chinese
white on beige paper
235 x 184
Signed, lower left: *F. Boucher f*
Provenance: Bosman
Exhibited: Boucher, 1932, no. 7
Lent by The Lazarus & Rosalie Phillips Family Collection

The drawing's subject is obscure, but the costumes and background seem to indicate an episode from the history of the
ancient Orient, possibly from the story of Cyrus the Great. The
suggestion of a columned palace hall with its richly draped cur-
tains, the soldiers in the left background, carrying their standards
and the soldier in the plumed helmet in the left foreground, are
all reminiscent of Boucher's *Continence of Scipio* studies (pls.
88–90), but it must be remembered that costumes and *mise-en-
scène* were very similar for all subjects drawn from antiquity. A
turban and draped, embroidered gown suggested the Orient; a
plumed helmet and spears denoted Greece or Rome.

92
Venus and Adonis

Black and white chalk on faded blue paper
315 x 218
Signed and dated at lower left: *F. Boucher 1767*
Provenance: Renouard; Thibaudeau (sale, Paris, Apr. 25, 1857, no. 696);[1] Magne; Heseltine; Joseph E. Widener
Bibliography: Portalis, I, p. 40; Goncourt, pp. 203, 204; Heseltine, 1900, no. 15; Michel, no. 633-634; H. Cohen, *Guide de l'Amateur de Livres à gravures du XVIIIe siècle,* Paris, 1912, col. 772; Heseltine, 1913, no. 13, repr.; S. de Ricci, *A Check-List of the More Important French Illustrated Books of the Eighteenth Century,* Philadelphia, 1923, p. 21
Exhibited: London, "National Loan Exhibition," 1909–1910, no. 76
Lent by the National Gallery of Art, Widener Collection

Among the drawings which Boucher contributed as illustrations to the edition of Ovid's *Metamorphoses* which appeared in a translation by the Abbé Banier (published between 1767 and 1771), was one of *Venus and Adonis,* engraved by Jean Massard. The episode in Book X, Fable XII, tells the story of the goddess Venus (Aphrodite) who fell deeply in love with the beautiful youth Adonis. He loved hunting, but Venus feared that he might be killed during the chase and begged him to hunt only animals that would not prove dangerous. He did not heed her warnings and met his tragic end in the form of a wild boar. The engraving by Massard is rather mediocre when compared with Boucher's drawing and hardly does justice to the attractive design for the illustration.

1. A collection of 127 drawings, presumably the original designs for the engravings for the 1767 Ovid, were in the Thibaudeau sale. Boucher's original nine drawings were sold in a separate group, as nos. 692-701.

93

Aurora and Cephalus

Brown chalk
325 x 219
Signed at lower right, *f Boucher f*
Provenance: Renouard; Thibaudeau (sale, Paris, Apr. 25,
1857, no. 695); Magne; Heseltine; Joseph E. Widener
Bibliography: Portalis, I, p. 40; Goncourt, pp. 203, 204;
Heseltine, 1900, no. 11, repr.; Michel, no. 453; H. Cohen,
Guide de l'Amateur de Livres à graveurs du XVIIIe siècle,
Paris, 1912, col. 772; Heseltine, 1913, no. 5, repr.; S. de Ricci,
*A Check-List of the More Important French Illustrated
Books of the Eighteenth Century,* Philadelphia, 1923; n.p.;
I. Moskowitz and A. Mongan, *Great Drawings of All Time,*
New York, 1962, III, no. 697, repr.; Vallery-Radot, pl. 62
Exhibited: London, "National Loan Exhibition," 1909–1910,
no. 71
Lent by the National Gallery of Art, Widener Collection

Three poets of antiquity, Homer, Vergil and Ovid, furnished most of the secular themes for European artists during the past two thousand years. So many of Boucher's compositions are based on Ovidian themes that one is prompted to examine the reasons for the Latin poet's appeal to the eighteenth century. Characterized by a seventeenth century French poet as *"le plus gentil et le plus ingénieux de tous les poètes grecs et latins,"* Ovid provided in his masterwork, the *Metamorphoses,* a stream of subject matter so vital that twenty centuries of artists and writers failed to exhaust it. Not only did Dante, Chaucer and Shakespeare, Ronsard, Corneille and André Chenier draw much of their inspiration from Ovid's extraordinary poem; the giants of the Renaissance, Raphael, Michelangelo and Titian; the Fontainebleau artists Rosso and Primaticcio, the baroque painters and finally the artists of the eighteenth century, and even those of the nineteenth, returned time and again to Ovidian themes for some of their most beautiful compositions. In our own day, Maillol and Picasso illustrated Ovid's poems, while contemporary French and English writers translated them.

An English scholar lists the qualities in Ovid which appealed to young poets: "his fertility in invention, his power of conjuring up vivid pictures, his unphilosophic gusto, his preoccupation with love, and his knowledge of the human heart."[1] Are these not the very qualities one finds so attractive in Boucher? Do they perhaps account for the strong affinity between the poet and the painter? For Boucher made use of the Ovidian myths long before the well-known translation of the *Metamorphoses* by Abbé Banier appeared in 1767; his *Aurora and Cephalus* at Nancy, for example, was done almost thirty-five years earlier than the Abbé's translation of the myth.

The illustration which Boucher furnished for the 1767 Ovid reverses the composition of the painting: the dawn goddess is placed at the left and the hunter Cephalus at the right. The *amorini,* holding the reins of the steeds which draw Aurora's chariot through the sky, try to arrest their course; these little winged messengers of love are the most spirited part of the composition, the figures of the goddess and the hunter being drawn with little verve or conviction.

Three years before his death, Boucher was still capable of painting and drawing with remarkable skill, but his hand often faltered and his imagination ran dry. He had illustrated the Aurora and Cephalus theme twice, in the magnificent painting of 1733 at Nancy, and in an oval composition dated 1764, intended as a design for a Gobelins tapestry. This latter painting was acquired by Louis XV and is now in the Louvre. The Washington drawing, commissioned as an illustration in Abbé Banier's translation, was engraved by Augustin de Saint-Aubin.

1. L. P. Wilkinson, *Ovid Surveyed,* Cambridge University, 1962, p. 12.

94

The Exodus of the Shepherds, or *The Caravan*

Black chalk heightened with white on prepared gray canvas
514 x 749
Provenance: Von Frey (sale, Paris, June 12–14, 1933, no. 1,
repr.)
Bibliography: Handbook of the Collections, Nelson Gallery-
Atkins Museum, Kansas City, 1959, p. 110, repr.
Exhibited: Kansas City, Nelson Gallery-Atkins Museum, "The
Century of Mozart," 1956, no. 127, fig. 20; Toronto, Ottawa,
San Francisco, New York, 1972–73, no. 15, pl. 9
Lent by the Nelson Gallery-Atkins Museum (Nelson Fund)

Like the two large paintings in the Museum of Fine Arts, Boston, *Halt at the Fountain* and *Returning from Market,* which Boucher painted toward the very end of his career, this drawing with its strong reminiscences of Benedetto Castiglione, has both pastoral elements and religious overtones. It is probably a late drawing, but the artist has crowded into it figures from his earliest compositions, when he was still under the influence of the Genoese master: animals like those in his early pastorals; the waving palm trees which occur in most of Boucher's Biblical scenes, and the mother holding an infant, a group he was to introduce into his rural idylls of the sixties and seventies. There are many enigmatic aspects to the drawing, as though the artist were struggling to express something not wholly clear in his mind. The figures crowding into the foreground, the procession of shepherds and flocks in the middle distance and the classical building in the background toward which a figure at the extreme left is pointing—all these can be read in various ways, but is it possible that they are meant to represent a Journey into the Promised Land?

95
La Danse Allemande

Brown chalk
337 x 223
Provenance: Anonymous sale, Paris, Feb. 19, 1869, no. 22;
Marmontel (sale, Paris, Jan. 25–26, 1883, no. 49); Léon
Michel-Levy (sale, Paris, June 17–18, 1925, no. 35, repr.);
Léon Lowenstein (sales, Paris, Dec. 17, 1935, no. 19; and
Paris, Mar. 7–8, 1938, no. 33, repr.)
Bibliography: Goncourt, p. 196; Michel, no. 1669; Ananoff,
no. 262, fig. 47
Exhibited: Boucher, 1932, no. 55; Copenhagen, Palais de
Charlottenborg, "Exposition de l'art français au XVIIIe siècle,"
1935, p. 99, no. 316
Lent by Arthur Ross

The *danse allemande,* "the most graceful and flowing court dance
of the period around 1700, came to the court of France from
Germany. The man and woman who were dance partners
always kept both hands joined. The man turned the woman in
various directions so that she circled and crossed under the arch
made by their hands and arms."[1] Although the dancers in
Boucher's drawing perform in a pastoral setting, it is doubtless
a stage setting, not a spot in some rural French village, for in the
background can be seen the sculptured figure of a female nude,
and the pedestal of what was probably a marble fountain. Because
of his work for the Opéra, Boucher was closely associated with
the composers and musicians of his time, among whom was the
celebrated Jean-Philippe Rameau, who wrote an exquisite piece
of music for the harpsichord, the *Allemande.* This may have
been the air to which the corps de ballet danced in one of the
opera-ballets composed by Rameau, and Boucher's drawing may
be the record of such a tableau, a moment seized and held in a
court performance. "It reflects a feeling for Nature," writes
Rameau's biographer, "for an artificial, dream-like nature, born
of the desires of the jaded court-dweller but infused with that
yearning which so readily pervades Rameau's music."[2] Boucher's
drawing, lightly sketched in brown chalk, was engraved by
Demarteau in sanguine, and dated 1768 (Leymarie, no. 203).

1. N. Lloyd, *The Golden Encyclopedia of Music,* New York, 1968, p. 15.
2. Girdlestone, *Jean-Philippe Rameau,* New York, 1965, p. 180.

96
Head of a Young Woman
Black chalk heightened with white and touches of pastel on
beige paper
254 x 156
Glomy stamp, lower right (Lugt 1085)
Provenance: Knaus (sale, Berlin, Oct. 30, 1917, no. 20)
Lent by Mrs. Herbert N. Straus

Perhaps more than any other artist of his day, Boucher strove to create an ideal of feminine grace and charm, and if a *tête de femme* or *tête de jeune fille* was based on an actual model, it quickly became a generalized type in which all individual features were abandoned, and whose sole function was to please the eye of the beholder.

Why so many heads of women? Demarteau alone engraved at least forty, in as many different poses. They are not portraits, nor do they show any suggestion of sensuality; their only aim is to express a loveliness which is sometimes merely pretty, but at other times verges on the austere, like the classicizing *Head of a Young Woman* in the Straus Collection. Seen in profile, her hair drawn back in classical severity, she stands for one type of feminine perfection in Boucher's idealized world: a combination of physical and spiritual grace.

Is the answer to our question, then, that Boucher drew so many heads of women because he attempted to create an ideal? Or is it perhaps to be found in one of the philosophic concepts of his day, surely familiar to him: that the quest for happiness is the duty of man? A modern historian paraphrases this idea: "of all the verities in existence, the only important ones were those that helped to make us happy . . . in short, man had but one moral duty, and that was to live a happy life."[1] Loveliness was pleasing; women's heads, embodying more than mere prettiness, became metaphors of beauty. And the contemplation of beauty must surely result in happiness. Could such reasoning have been the underlying motive for Boucher's constant preoccupation with heads of women?

1. P. Hazard, *European Thought in the Eighteenth Century*, p. 15.

97
Head of a Young Girl

Black chalk heightened with white and colored chalks, on
buff paper
285 x 222
Inscribed lower left: *f. Boucher* with *paraphe*
Provenance: Mary Benjamin Rogers
Lent anonymously

An eighteenth century traveler is said to have found, in a Swiss
picture dealer's shop, a group of nine pastels of women's heads
by Boucher which, he said, might have been called *le Cabinet
des Beautés,* for they were life studies of the nine most beautiful
models then reigning in Paris.[1] The Goncourts feel, in fact, that
most of Boucher's heads of women in pastel or colored crayons
are *"des portraits déguisés,"* and that under the guise of idealized
portraits the artist was drawing the likeness of ladies whose iden-
tities were known only to their friends or lovers.[2] This may well
have been true of Boucher's fellow artists, Nattier, Tocqué, La
Tour, Drouais, Perronneau, all of whom drew heads of women
in charcoal, *trois crayons* and pastel which were recognizably
portraits of ladies known and unknown. In Boucher's case, there
was a lack of interest in portraiture (perhaps because portraiture
as such was not as highly esteemed by the Académie as other
genres of painting), and a tendency to turn a woman's face
into a pretty ornament, as he managed to do with this *Head of
a Young Girl*; individuation of features rarely exist. This generalized treatment has made it difficult to identify the women he
portrayed, with the result that even the portrait of one of his
daughters was for a long time taken to be that of Madame de
Pompadour.[3] As for his own wife, or the Murphy sisters who
served him as models, it is easier to establish their identity by
their nude bodies than their pretty, expressionless faces.

The medium used in the drawing of *Head of a Young Woman*
deserves special mention, for it is one Boucher was happiest
with—black and white and colored chalks—"delicate and fragile
as the dust on a butterfly's wings, in shades of an almost infinite
variety, like the colors of the rainbow."[4]

1. Goncourt, p. 174.
2. Goncourt, p. 174.
3. G. Monnier, *Pastels XVIIème et XVIIIème siècles,* Paris, 1972, no. 26.
4. M. Sérullaz, Preface to *Pastels XVIIème et XVIIIème siècles,* p. 4.

98
Head of a Girl

Black and red chalk
163 x 123
Inscribed, bottom left of mat: *f. boucheé*
Provenance: Earl of Dalhousie (Lugt 717[a])
Exhibited: Williamstown, Clark Art Institute, "Drawings of
the 16th, 17th and 18th Centuries," 1965, no. 34, and "Drawings
by G. B. Tiepolo, G. D. Tiepolo, and Other 18th-Century
Masters from the Institute's Collection," 1970–71
Bibliography: Baudicour, II, p. 38; E. Haverkamp-Begemann,
S. D. Lawder and C. W. Talbot, Jr., *Drawings from the
Clark Art Institute,* New Haven and London, 1964, no. 34,
pl. 35
Lent by the Sterling and Francine Clark Art Institute

This drawing may be a preliminary study, possibly from life, for
a much more finished portrait of a girl, done *aux trois crayons,*
which was formerly in the Léon Michel-Lévy Collection (sale,
Paris, June 17–18, 1925, pl. 29) and was engraved by Demarteau
as *Tête de Femme* (Leymarie, no. 217). The original drawing
had belonged to Boucher's patron, Madame d'Azaincourt. Still
another study of the same model was formerly in the Koenigs
Collection.[1] A rather poor copy of the Williamstown drawing
was in the Laffon Sale (Zurich, Apr. 7–8, 1938). The *Head of
a Girl* in Williamstown is beyond question the freshest and most
appealing version.

1. Exhibited, Rotterdam, Museum Boymans, "Meesterwerken uit Vier
Eeuwen, 1400-1800," 1938, no. 235, fig. 300.

99
The Presentation in the Temple

Pen and brown wash, heightened with white, over black chalk
322 x 198
Arched at top
Provenance: Heseltine
Bibliography: Heseltine, 1900, no. 16, repr.; Michel, no. 819;
Heseltine, 1913, no. 4, repr.; T. Sizer, "Drawings by Boucher
and Fragonard," *Bulletin of The Cleveland Museum of Art,*
Jan. 1926, pp. 5–8, repr. on the cover; Ananoff, no. 651; L.
Declaux, in *Great Drawings of the Louvre Museum, the
French Drawings,* (M. Sérullaz, ed.), New York, 1968, ment.
no. 50; Jean-Richard, p. 104; Rosenberg, p. 138
Exhibited: Palm Beach, Society of the Four Arts, "French
Masterpieces of the Eighteenth Century," 1952–1953, no. 16;
Paris, Orangerie, 1958, no. 37, pl. 46
Lent by The Cleveland Museum of Art
Leonard C. Hanna Jr. Collection

One of the very last drawings Boucher did, shortly before he died, is *The Presentation in the Temple* in the Cabinet des Dessins of the Louvre, an oil sketch signed F B and dated 1770.[1] Except for a few details, the composition is essentially the same as the Cleveland drawing. Two other versions are recorded in eighteenth century collections, that of the painter Aved in 1766 and of Boucher's patron, Blondel d'Azaincourt in 1770. It would seem, therefore, that the subject had preoccupied Boucher for a number of years, and that he attempted, until the end of his life, to paint an imposing altarpiece based on the sketches in pen and ink, wash and oil. Lise Duclaux draws attention to the Rembrandtesque quality of the Louvre *Présentation,* a striking aspect of the Cleveland drawing as well, and a reminder that Boucher himself collected the works of the great Dutch master, retaining them in his studio until his death. In the sale of Boucher's effects in 1771, a *grisaille* painting *The Presentation in the Temple* (no. 81) is considered the final step in the project for what was undoubtedly to be an important altarpiece.

1. See Jean-Richard, no. 113, pl. 24.

100

*Design for a Frontispiece Surmounted by the
Sacred Monogram IHS*

Pen and black ink with gray wash
170 x 229
Signed lower center: *françois Boucher inv. del*
Provenance: Beurdeley (Lugt 421); Stieglitz; The Hermitage
(sale, Leipzig, May 4, 1932, no. 11)
Lent by The Metropolitan Museum of Art, Purchase,
Gift of Anne and Carl Stern

This title page, probably intended for a work of a religious nature, is nevertheless done in the rococo style associated with more worldly designs. Boucher, it would appear, insisted on creating an attractive image no matter what the nature of the subject. The drawing may also have served as a design for a commemorative tablet containing an epitaph. Such plaques were frequently affixed to the walls of churches and private chapels.

This catalog was produced by the Editor's Office, National
Gallery of Art, Washington. Printed by the Meriden Gravure
Company, Meriden, Connecticut. Set in Linotype Granjon by the
Monotype Composition Company, Inc., Baltimore, Maryland.
Display type set in Nicolas Cochin by Harlowe Typography, Inc.
The text paper is 80 pound Mohawk Superfine, and the cover
80 pound Mohawk Superfine.
Designed by Valerie Hardy, Washington.